What Muses Do

Edward Bowman and Aurora Dawn

DEDICATION

This book is dedicated to my best friend, Aurora Dawn. She goes through her life unaware of her own perfection, how beautiful a person she is, and how loved she is, but she is most special to all she interacts with. Without her in my life, my inspiration would be gone. As usual, since she is my Muse, these poems are both for her, and about her.

CONTENTS

ACKNOWLEDGMENTS

My first acknowledgement is to GOD. It is HE who gave me life and created me to love the arts and writing. HE also gave me a romantic view of life, and with that, a great pair of eyes for seeing beauty in the world around me.

Secondly, I have to acknowledge the effort of my Muse in this. While I am pretty sure she is actually a woman, there are times I wonder if she is a heavenly being of some sort who has come down from a beautiful, ethereal plane to walk among us and inspire love and art wherever she goes.

Preface

When I started writing poetry, I really never intended to actually publish any books. I had written some stories and poetry in the past just for personal fulfillment, but when my muse came into my life, the purpose of most of my writing became to show how I felt about her, the beauty she caused me to see, or just to please her.

The genesis of this book was the first poem in the book, "What Muses Do". I wrote it about a year ago, and sent it to her. She loved it, and told me that needed to be the title of my next book. In fact, I think she might have actually proclaimed it. I put it with a sister poem, "Calliope", such that it shows what muses do from both points of view.

So, I continued writing for her, and found something interesting had happened. I found that while much of my writing was about the beauty I see in the world, there was also some of it that dealt with some of the darkness we find in life. When I looked at the cause of this, I found that the darker content happened when I was worried about her, worried about how she felt about me, worried I had hurt her feelings, or otherwise felt like I was less important to her than I want to be. Most of these times happened when I was very tired, and really had little to do with her changing how she feels, or her approach to me. I don't think that will ever change, as what we have is profound. However, my brain would start poring over different scenarios when I was really tired, or my defenses were otherwise down. I would find things like loneliness, feeling unwanted, and sadness creeping in.

So, although unintended, it came out that I had poems about the darkness that all mankind faces, but more poems about the light that all mankind seeks, which is being loved, be it by GOD or another human being, and then a few poems about our journey between them. We then decided to actually divide the book this way: The Dark, the Light, and the Journey mankind makes between them.

As a final note, I wanted to explain the last poem, in which I shut down the "forge" of my writing. I had written a poem that I thought was pretty good. It was about how beautiful a woman with child is, as it is so special to be blessed to carry a life inside her, right below her heart. I also touched on how blessed was the man by a woman that consented to make a life with him. I had used the metaphor of a gardener to describe this, and wrote about how she lovingly tended to all the needs of the growing plants that she loved. Well, to make a long story shorter, the Muse did not like this poem. She took it in a way that I had not intended it, and, it just did not really sit well with her. Believe it or not, this is something an artist actually controls. Art is, of course, open to whatever interpretation the viewer chooses, but the artist is responsible to establish the context, or framework, within which this interpretation takes place. So, in the same way that if I had written a poem about a gently flowing river as a metaphor for the eternal flow of time, and I have readers wondering why I am writing about hot air balloon races, I had clearly failed in establishing the intended framework for interpretation.

I realized that since I had missed the mark so badly with the poem, I should probably take a break to work on the publishing process, and pick the pen back up another day. As it turns out, this made me end up with another 100 poems or so, just like the first book, "The Modern Muse".

I thought it was important to relate to the reader, both how the book came to be , and a brief insight into my creative process, and the Muse's part in that.

Thank you for picking up this book to read, and I really hope that you enjoy the content nearly as much as my Muse does.

-Edward Bowman, November 2018.

Preface: Addendum

After this book was published, I had some feedback from some of the readers, as well as an editor. The upshot of their feedback is that they were hopeful for two things. One, that the poem, "Come Back to Me" could be added to such that there was more detail about what happened in France, and events surrounding what the poem described, and two, that the poem about gravid women which the Muse interpreted in an unintended way be published.

Well, let me start with the second question first. I have no plans of publishing this poem, though, of course, I still have it. Perhaps after I die, one of my children – or some other interested party – will find it and publish it. I won't care, because I will have shuffled off this mortal coil. I WILL, however put in a different poem I wrote called, "A Kiss" in the last section of the book instead.

As to the first question, I am making the poem, "Come Back to Me" one part of a five poem offering called Agincourt. This will serve to explain what this poem is about. I had originally planned to include these in one of the last two books in this series, but realized that as my plan for the last two books became finalized, the format of them would not allow the rest of this story to be told in them.

I don't usually get this detailed about a creative process, but I will do so here, although briefly. This poem came from a series of dreams I had where I was back in Wales. I was on a hill overlooking the sea, and the Muse came up to me though she was dressed in garb that was popular over 600 years ago. We recognized each other, but as we were from different times, there was a bit of strangeness and disconnect about it. That it is how it all came about, and the poem, "Agincourt" will detail the entire set of events that occurred in my dreams.

-Edward Bowman, January 2021

WHAT MUSES DO

She put her hand within my own.
It seems from me she drew,
My sleeping creativity,
And put it in full view.

She put her hand upon my cheek,
And showed me something true.
Inspiring me by who she is,
Her light in me came through.

She took my heart within her hands,
With eyes of greenish hue.
She smiled and whispered in my ear,
"This is what muses do"

CALLIOPE

One time I saw Terpsichore,
So beautifully inspiring dance,
But found her art called not to me,
Though she is worthy of romance.

So then I sought the wisest muse,
Her beauty only thus surpassed
By power of her mind profuse.
I sought with her my fate to cast.

The trials of my search are found,
In other writings by my hand,
But finally found I muse renowned,
And found to flame my passions fanned.

She touched my heart and thus inspired,
A prophet for her poetry.
Our closeness showed she is desired,
And all men love Calliope.

DIVISION I: THE DARKNESS ALL MEN FACE

THE STRUGGLE OF MANKIND AGAINST OUR

OWN FALLEN NATURE

Edward Bowman

A USEFUL MAN

I dreamed I to a rock was chained,
Upon the cliff so desolate,
Where once before you had remained,
And saved me from my prison fate.

Accusers stood around me there,
And struck me with their fists of rage.
I looked for anyone to care,
But no one cared of any age.

The men all wore a hooded robe.
I could not make out any face,
Fear was the point of their wardrobe,
To match the aura of this place.

The lead accuser spoke to me,
And said in a sepulchral tone,
That I should not try to be free.
Since my fate is to be alone.

He said "You are a useful man,
But not a man one would desire.
You being wanted's not the plan,
So you should not seek passion's fire.

You're useful to your loves protect,
And your capacity for love,
Designed as vast by architect,
Who looks upon you from above.

You're useful to take care of all,
The needs of others all around,
But this is also your downfall,
For this has not desire unbound.

Your children grown, you raised them well,
But strong, they you no longer need.
And she with whom you chose to dwell,
Seems now to cut and watch you bleed.

Those with whom you have been in love,
Have also cared and loved you too,
But usefulness, replacement of,
The love they might have felt for you.

All five have known you are complex,
And smarter than the average bear.
Romantic and not pushing sex,
All five wish that you still were there.

But you have chained yourself so fast,
You cannot see how they see you.
Your eyes from light are now downcast.
You think you don't deserve love true.

Ironically, how at the end,
When you at last shall pass away,
So many will their mem'ries send,
And show their love from yesterday.

And as the dream faded away,
I realized things were not to be.
My usefulness holds love at bay,
I'll die with no one wanting me.

APOLOGY

I stood upon a hill in Wales,
And saw a maiden there.
A filigree of silver pure,
Adorned her golden hair.

I knew her as my dearest friend,
And was so close to her.
She inspiration and respect,
Within my heart did stir.

Her eyes were limpid pools of green,
That took the morning sun,
And played with glorious golden rays,
A promise of love won.

Her dress was of the purest white,
Her lips a luscious pink.
All this with gentle curves displayed,
Conspired to make me think.

That even though I held her in,
The highest of regard,
Could my control of self be crushed,
Like rubble in a yard?

I realized that it never could,
Because she would be hurt,
If ever I stepped over bounds,
That were set up by her.

I smiled as she came towards me,
As always in the past.
She ever was a joy to see,
Each time exceeding last!

'Twas then I saw her frown at me,
And start to turn away.
She whispered that she'd just come back,
Upon a diff'rent day.

I realized then that all my thoughts,
Within my head a crowd,
Had made a bid for freedom and,
I had said some out loud.

I knew I'd disappointed her,
And closed my eyes to stay,
Revulsion growing for myself,
And ultimate dismay.

I opened up my tearing eyes,
And sought with her to speak,
But she'd already gone away.
So I left lonely peak.

I went into my manor house,
And took my fav'rite bow.
Then I went out into the yard,
And let one arrow go.

I'd hoped that speeding arrow would,
Take with it misery,
And bury it deep in the ground,
Where it I could not see.

So over manor house it flew,
Toward ancient wooded stream,
But from where no-one should have been,
I heard a woman scream.

I ran to copse as fast I could.
Who was it I had harmed?
'Twas then I saw my arrow had,
Nicked her on her fair arm.

The dress which up til now had been,
As white as driven snow,
Was red due to her precious blood,
Which from her arm did flow.

Through burning tears, I bound her wound,
Then crashed down to a knee.
I wished the Earth would open up,
And to its depths take me.

But she came near and bore me up,
And brushed away my tears.
She said that she forgave me, and,
Disbanded all my fears.

She knew that there was malice none,
Nor was there ill intent,
That I should cause her any hurt,
Was just an accident.

She said that everything's OK,
And from me did depart.
Her graciousness to my sad soul,
A balm unto my heart.

Should I ever forgive myself,
Or carry to my end,
The guilt of having shot my bow,
And wounding dearest friend?

BEING MISSED

As I read this, I know that I,
Am bound to someone else's soul.
Together, we eternal lie,
As two halves of a greater whole.

I close my eyes as tears well up,
For physically we are apart.
My love has filled my spirit's cup,
And sits enthroned within my heart.

Kind fate has to us both decreed,
That interlaced we'll always be,
And our love never can recede,
For of one spirit both are we.

I wish that we together were,
For life is fullest side by side.
The bond of soul mates is so pure,
One cannot true affection hide.

I sorely miss this person who,
Will brighten up the darkest day.
I know my love misses me too,
For seconds seem like months away.

Though for a time my lover bides
By circumstance apart from me,
God's wisdom to my soul confides
That missed is the best place to be.

.

DESIRE

Come, sit beside me in your chair,
And I'll tell you of great despair.
A story started long ago,
A tale filled with both pain and woe.

It started when he first was born,
Upon an icy Winter morn.
He was quite blessed from up above,
With great capacity for love.

His childhood was filled with light,
With worries none, and happy quite,
But parents almost on a whim,
Revealed they had not wanted him.

It seems an odd dichotomy,
That they could still love one as he,
But at the same time want him not,
For this he any answer sought.

So, as he lived he fell in love,
But only with few women of,
High quality for it was writ,
That once he loved, he'd never quit.

Each one he loved, and they loved him,
With light he'd fill them to the brim,
But circumstance would intervene,
And due to something unforeseen,

The women, in their comfort, found,
Their confidence became unbound,
And knew he always would be there,
Protecting them and showing care,

They soon would drift upon life's stream,
To find themselves another dream.
He smiled at their happiness,
Rememb'ring fondly their caress.

In time, though he was kind to them,
Not one spared many thoughts for him.
Though they might seek him when they hurt,
For he would all their pain divert.

He loved them all, but he was blind,
At first to truth with cut unkind.
It must be told, the day was grim,
When this truth was revealed to him.

Throughout his life, he loved had been,
And though he tried time and again,
From birth until his lonely death,
He realized with his dying breath,

No one had really wanted him,
And closed he both eyes grown so dim.
He could not stop the flow of tears.
As he remembered all the years,

He'd spent in love but wanted not,
He conjured up a final thought
And as he passed into the night,
He wished he'd known true love's pure light.

FINAL WISHES

I wish I could have better been,
As someone made for you.
I hope you know I did my best,
To show you something new.

I wish that I had not been shy,
But still I do perceive,
What seems as shy is so that you,
No disrespect receive.

I wish that I had finished all,
The books I strove to write.
So you might always know that you,
Had been my Earthly light.

I wish that all your days are filled,
With light and love so free,
And also hope that for some time,
You will remember me.

I wish that ere my windows close,
And life light finally fails,
That you know how much you were loved,
And this will fill your sails.

I wish it were I did not know,
The truth of life it seems.
That wishes mostly useless are,
Except within our dreams.

FULFILLED IN HIM

I heard your plaintive cries for help,
While I was close beside,
A river swollen to a flood.
I ran to where you cried.

I pulled you from the current fast,
And nearby laid you down.
I made sure that you breathed again.
I would not let you drown.

You shivered with the wet and cold.
I gave my coat to you.
I covered you and made you warm,
Your lips no longer blue.

I made a fire upon the bank
So you could feel it's heat.
Then used the fire to cook a meal,
So you and I could eat.

'Twas then you turned your smile at me,
And all my walls destroyed.
I needed no defense from you
Your spirit filled my void.

You came and sat beside me then,
And leaned against my side.
I put my arm around you to
Protect you as you dried.

We sat beside the river there,
Upon the edge of sleep,
The water sang a lullaby,
With current fast and deep.

I felt so very close to you,
Your breath upon my cheek,
A woman of great quality,
That every man will seek.

When you had regained all your strength,
There came to us a man.
You seemed to know him for you rose,
And took him by the hand.

I saw you walk away with him,
And as I rose, I tripped.
Upon the cloak you'd left behind,
And on wet stones I slipped.

You did not notice that I fell,
Into the water cold.
I could not gain my footing there,
And water o'er me rolled.

Happy was I that my hot tears,
The water washed away,
So if you happened to look back,
They would not me betray.

I cried not for impending doom,
But that I'd never know.
The beauty of a life with you,
We both with love aglow.

As water flowed over my head,
And my keen vision blurred.
I watched you both together walk,
Away without a word.

I wished for your fulfillment, and
In happiness to be,
Alive and living life in full,
Even if without me.

I knew that I would die that day.
I did not try to swim.
I realized I was happy for,
You were fulfilled in him.

I CANNOT HELP BUT WEEP

I'm disappointed in myself,
You might think I am cheap.
I missed a chance to buy you boots,
I cannot help but weep.

I want to show you my regard,
How my heart you can keep
But I was absent for your need.
I cannot help but weep.

I wish that I could perfect be,
But my flaws run so deep.
In contrast to perfection yours,
I cannot help but weep.

I wish that I could turn back time,
And back an hour leap.
I should have taken care of you.
I cannot help but weep.

It was an act of ignorance,
My intellect asleep,
But still, another moment lost,
I cannot help but weep.

Since I am quite impulsive but,
I look before I leap,
Why could I not have acted then?
I cannot help but weep.

I'm sure it doesn't bother you,
But I now sorrow reap.
I hate to disappoint you so.
I cannot help but weep.

I WILL BE THERE

I wish that I could make you smile.
Your sadness, like tears, bring the rain.
The sun is darkened all the while,
Until you feel good once again.

I'm sending you my fondest thoughts,
And all my feelings good and true.
I long ago connected dots,
My answered prayers are found in you.

Your gentle sobs a poet hears.
I sit beside you in my mind.
Please use my shoulder for your tears.
And maybe even solace find.

If you could just a moment take,
And bottle your most precious tears.
And save this cordial for man's sake.
They would heal any wounds or fears.

Though I know life can be quite hard,
I wonder if I failed, you see,
To show you highest of regard,
And that you mean the world to me.

In times like these just deeply breathe,
And gently close your pretty eyes.
Let memories fond in your mind wreathe,
And turn your face up to the skies.

And then, perhaps you'll understand.
As a breeze touches flaxen hair,
That if you but reach out your hand,
No matter what, I will be there.

LOVE POTION

I only want for her to feel,
About me how I feel for her.
I did not much my love conceal,
For her my passions are astir.

It's not that I objectified,
Her as a tool for pleasure mine.
My love for her is vast and wide,
Without condition nor decline.

I told her once, just how I felt,
But she to me no answer gave.
I rather would a blow been dealt,
That put me in an early grave.

So, I went to an alchemist,
To from him a love potion buy,
To give me something to assist,
Her love for me lest I should die.

He said, "You seek a potion rare.
How much would you give me for this?"
I said, "For cost I do not care,
So precious is her fleeting kiss."

He said, "I can offer advice,
And tell you things that you could do,
No potion, though, at any price,
Will make her fall in love with you.

You want a woman with freewill,
To choose to love you rather than,
Another person's love fulfill,
And choose to love a different man.

If magic could her strong will break,
Then she would not have made the choice,
If you could such an action take,
She would no longer have a voice.

She would be changed, and would not be,
The woman that you're thinking of,
Whatever, then, she felt for you,
Would be most foul, and not be love.

For your part you can treat her well,
And for her love in secret pine,
Imprisoned in a painful hell,
Your love to pain will you consign.

If she is of a vintage rare,
Then silently just wait for her,
When she needs you, for her be there,
Though love might not within her stir.

The other option quicker be,
To find yourself a woman new,
There's many, and, of them, you see,
One may well fall in love with you."

I thanked him for his sage advice,
And said I'd stop and talk again.
I said no other would suffice,
And she is worth more than my pain.

I thought of what he'd said to me,
And knew there could not be on Earth,
A different woman I could see,
Of half her caliber and worth.

So I went back and got in bed,
And felt my tears flow freely down,
With many thoughts within my head,
And sought to clamp emotion down.

But soon from me, there came a wail,
Inhuman as a beast's might be,
I knew that hope would not prevail.
She'd never fall in love with me.

PINING

She cried herself to sleep that night,
And woke with tears still in her eyes.
He raised her to so high a height,
That far below her were the skies.

She wished she had just once held him,
And let him feel the love she felt.
His love had filled her to the brim,
But they a fateful hand were dealt.

They both mates were of other's soul,
But he from her untimely ripped.
She lost the half that made her whole,
Despair at her now surely nipped.

Through unstopped tears she cried aloud,
Her breath was ragged as she wept.
She whispered as her head she bowed,
And asked of him whose soul she kept.

"Why did I never let you see
Nor let you know how you'd be missed?
Why could I not your lover be,
And let your lips not be unkissed?

In heaven where you now must dwell,
Will you not spare a thought for me?
Will you not come to me and tell,
How I can live? What is the key?"

She heard his voice upon the wind.
Her fears dissolved like tears in rain.
She felt him to her side descend.
He banished both despair and pain.

**"While I still lived I knew your love,
And not in heaven I reside.
Until we both are called above,
I always will be at your side"**

SLIPPING

I walked along the path with you,
We held each other's hand.
About to gain the mountain top,
Fate did something unplanned.

We walked beside the highest cliff,
With me on the outside.
So high that clouds were far below,
And path was not so wide.

I thought that we had felt the same,
And walked in harmony.
Alas that I misunderstood,
And tripped on what can't be.

Our feet got tangled in mid stride.
I stumbled seeking if,
My answer heard, I kept you safe,
But I fell off the cliff.

Over the side, I caught myself,
By grabbing at a rock.
I hung there between hea'en and Earth,
And grip I tried to lock.

I could not see you any more.
I tried to quell my fears.
Were you still on the path above?
Would you experience tears?

I thought about my options, and,
My gen'ral worthlessness.
I knew I in no way deserved,
Your light with which you bless.

I want you to be happy, and,
I wish I were a part,
I hoped you might come to the edge,
For man within your heart.

I thought about the ground below.
I was too high to see.
'Twas then an inspiration hit,
Concerning gravity.

I fixed your image in my mind,
As I began to slip.
I would you hold all the way down,
I could not hold my grip.

I pictured that the ground below,
Was you drawing me nigh,
For gravity I knew that it,
Would want me 'til I die.

SOLITAIRE

There is a game named solitaire,
That one must play alone.
To win, you must play every card,
But outcome is unknown.

If one has not the proper cards,
In certain order true,
There is no way to win the game,
No matter what you do.

Some people play this game in life,
And don't have anyone.
They are alone and bitterly,
Know this game can't be won.

Sometimes no matter what one's skill,
Nor what they deign to try,
They do not have the proper cards,
And can't win ere they die.

THE ERRANT ARROW

I am a Bowman of renown,
And got a brand new bow.
I had not felt this way in years,
And so I had to know.

How would it feel to draw the string,
And feel the bow arms bend?
So then I nocked an arrow, and
It down the range did send.

At first it seemed on target, then,
It drifted slightly wide.
It hit the target's hardened edge,
Deflecting to the side.

I heard her sudden shriek of pain,
Before I saw her there.
My arrow had passed through her arm.
Her blood was everywhere.

I dropped my bow and ran to her,
And cradled wounded arm.
Through tears I bound the wound I'd made,
Where I had caused her harm.

With sunken heart I told her that
I never would intend,
To ever do an action which
Would hurt my dearest friend.

I felt hate for myself arise,
As she cried in her pain.
Her precious tears that I made flow,
Adjudged me most profane.

I wished the ground would swallow me,
I would prefer to die.
Rather than be responsible
For pain that made her cry.

I asked that she in fondest thoughts
Set me free in so far
That I had shot an arrow false,
And wounded morning star.

She made no answer, but she looked
At me with liquid eyes.
She bravely tried to hide the hurt,
Which could not be disguised.

She held out both her arms to me,
Where she laid on the ground.
I bent and gently picked her up
With feelings most profound.

I carried her from that grave field
To whereso healing be.
My heart broke as I laid her down.
She had forgiven me.

THE MOONLESS NIGHT

It was upon a moonless night,
I watched you walk away.
The darkness brought with it despair.
I knew not what to say.

We think about the languages,
Wherein we love might feel.
We think of gifts and spending time,
And touch that is ideal.

When you were ill, I understood,
And sought only to be.
Someone who might take care of you,
Though you might not see me.

It might have been a bowl of soup,
Or comfort in soft words.
Perhaps just checking in on you,
For strength that undergirds.

Compassion stirred from deep within,
When you felt near to death.
I wished I could take fear from you,
And give you back your breath.

I thought I knew just why it was,
There was no time for me.
With fell affliction in your lungs,
You could not sicker be.

And then, upon that fateful night,
You went to river's bend.
The plague did not stop what you want,
Such precious time to spend.

I think you did not mean it so,
But something became clear.
I am of far less worth than him,
For you hold him most dear.

I don't blame you for such a choice,
You should feel what you feel.
I'm glad that you can happy be,
And have a love that's real.

The struggle that now comes to me,
Is nothing that you did.
For you're perfection come to Earth,
And of all darkness rid.

What am I fighting as we speak?
A mind that won't shut down.
It's fighting that which must be true,
A battle of renown.

On one side is that I am good,
But still a human man.
The other, my unworthiness,
Though I'm part of some plan.

Yet in the end it matters not,
I know that which is true.
Whate'er befalls, it will not change,
Just what I feel for you.

Edward Bowman

THE OLD SAILOR

For many years I've sailed these seas,
And weathered oft the violent storm,
I've found safe harbors, and at ease,
I shelter there both safe and warm.

But commerce changed as time went on,
With newer ships demanding berth,
At last I found my need was gone,
And I, to them, had lost my worth.

I sailed and searched and thought that I,
Had found a port that needed me.
To be wanted the reason why,
I brave the dark and stormy sea.

I thought about the journey's end,
How people there would show me love,
And with them all my life would blend,
With happiness I knew not of.

As I sailed to the harbor new,
A storm began to scream and rage,
The gale and wind my poor ship blew,
I hoped I might my fears assuage.

I saw a lighthouse on the shore,
That marked a sheltered harbor there.
I fought against the tempest's roar,
And smiled at the harbor rare.

My happiness, it seems was short,
For as I made the final turn,
And headed for safe berth in port,
My rudder broke and wrecked my stern.

My vessel smashed into the rocks,
I knew that fate I could not fight,
I died before I found the docks,
Just grateful that I'd seen the light.

TUCKING IN

Although apart, together we,
At all times share a mystic bond.
Does she know that I'll always be,
Without condition always fond?

Each night as she prepares for bed,
When sleep weighs down her pretty eyes,
I hint at things I have not said,
And wish her sweet dreams as her prize.

But since we are at night apart,
There are some times we cannot talk.
Yet we still know the other's heart,
And still on the same path we walk.

When lurkers make their presence known.
I see the late hour dim her light.
Does she know that she's not alone,
And still to her I said goodnight?

Sometimes when I am lost in thought,
And darkness on me presses down.
I fight but find I just cannot,
Without her light do aught but drown.

Yet still in hope I do abide,
For that is what she wants of me.
This seems to slow a downward slide.
I know I need her light to see.

This hope I have makes me go on,
And also does my feelings stir.
I wonder as I wait for Dawn,
If she knows that I think of her.

I know she always will be there,
Eternal as our bond has been.
She shows to me the greatest care,
And I will always tuck her in.

WHAT IF?

When I see you, and what you've done,
To bathe my life in bless-ed light,
I think on what we have begun,
And what so could have been my plight.

What if we two had never met?
Would I know that my world was gray?
Would I by beauty be beset,
And would my joy grow every day?

Would I know what it was I lost?
And would I still imagine you?
What to my soul would be the cost,
If your pure soul I never knew?

I fight back tears when I perceive,
How hollow life is wont to be,
Without a Muse to love receive,
And with no light for me to see.

I wonder in this train of thought,
If I am trapped inside a dream.
My fevered brain a woman wrought,
As perfect as the morning beam.

And even if this is a ruse,
Effected by my tortured brain,
You still will always be my Muse,
And I hope I'll see you again.

That being said, I need not know,
"What if", because you're here with me.
I always feel your warmest glow,
And know that you again I'll see.

DIVISION II: THE JOURNEY ALL MEN MAKE

THE JOURNEY MANKIND MAKES FROM THE

DARKNESS OF ISOLATION AND LONELINESS

TOWARDS THE LIGHT OF LOVE AND INCLUSION

Edward Bowman

AGINCOURT: THE DREAM

Last night I dreamed he came to me,
Upon the hill beside his house.
Where we would look upon the sea,
And seek how we might our fates chouse.

I noticed he was strangely dressed,
And seemed to not know where we were.
He spoke with voice both nice, but stressed,
And sought he with me to confer.

The tears welled up in both my eyes,
And, silently, slid down my face,
For looked he 'round and to the skies,
Then asked of me, "What is this place?"

I took his head within my hands,
And said, "You're back in Wales, my dear.
We stand on your ancestral lands,
Where you oft loved to draw me near.

From Pembrokeshire you went to war,
But now you have come back to me.
That you came back to our Welsh shore,
Gives me great hope I need to see."

He said, "I'm dreaming I'm in Wales,
But recognize this hillock not.
I recognize you, but details,
About you seem not what they ought."

My tears flowed more as I could see,
That he, conflicted in his soul,
Still loved but could not recall me,
Though we two halves of greater whole.

Then something happened worse than this.
I sobbed and knelt beside our tree,
He lost our language with a hiss,
And spoke in English odd to me.

I did not know it very well,
And understood not what he said.
He helped me up as if to quell,
My fear he was already dead.

With widened eyes but gentle tone,
He seemed to try to make me see,
That I was not in this alone.
Then faded he away from me.

I gasped and fell down to my knees,
I wished my mother wise where there.
'Twas then I felt the evening breeze,
That ran cold fingers through my hair.

I closed my eyes to fight my fears,
That he was now already dead.
My scream broke through my silent tears,
And I awoke upon my bed.

AGINCOURT: COME BACK TO ME

Your duty called you far away,
To fight in France for English King.
With failing hope, I wait each day,
And to this faintest hope I cling.

My mother tried to comfort me,
And said, " I know what's come to pass.
You're not the first princess you see,
Loved by a peer below your class.

I speak from my experience,
That love regards not class apart.
For though our culture takes offense,
You cannot fight what fills your heart.

As to your soldier, gone to war,
He and his family known so well,
As oft as you both met before,
I'm sure that you in his heart dwell.

Although he never love expressed,
His actions show his fond regard.
You should not be in such distress,
He told you not, your place to guard."

I felt the tears run down my face.
I said, "He once expressed his love.
'Twas hidden in a poem of grace,
Concealed in language from above.

But since society rebukes,
A love like this, though heaven sent,
For Thanes serve far below the Dukes,
We had to be with fate content.

I never told him his import,
And neither of my feelings true,
I fear he's died in foreign port,
Still unaware I loved him too"

My mother held me close to her,
With tears in both her queenly eyes,
"I think when such emotions stir,
You should this write and not disguise"

With parting touch she left me there,
With parchment, ink and turkey quill.
So you can see my soul is bare,
Though now, I fear you never will.

You seem to haunt most vivid dreams,
This makes me fear you have been slain.
Though things are different, so it seems,
I now draw every breath in pain.

You seem confused, and can't recall,
Some things that we have both held dear,
And then you cannot speak at all,
Our language. This fills me with fear.

My heart is breaking with the fact,
That not until sweet paradise,
Will I your eyes to me attract.
I'm not sure I can pay this price.

Since all that's left are dreams of you,
The next time that I see you there,
I'll give you this, though dreams aren't true,
So you might know my every prayer.

For all my life, you've been on guard,
And when the Dolmen scene occurred,
Almost within your own backyard,
I knew that something deeply stirred.

To close I wanted you to know,
That you are steady in my mind,
And every day, I miss you so,
For someone like you, I'll not find.

So every day to field I'll go,
Close by your house, next to the sea,
And wait with hope, so faint, I know,
That you will still return to me.

AGINCOURT: DELIVERY

Last week I had the dream again,
Wherein my Muse stood on a hill.
I went to her, to thus begin,
A conversation seeming real.

She beautiful, but oddly clothed,
In wondrous dress from long ago.
Effect the same, for nothing loathed,
Survived her light and loving glow.

She ran across the hill to me,
But stopped just short of an embrace.
Though different, 'tis my Muse I see.
She still the same in form and face.

She smiled and said, "It's really you!
I know not how this thing can be.
For while the same, you're different too,
But still my truest love I see.

To you I must the message give,
A letter that you soon shall see.
It is for you, if you still live.
I need you to come back to me."

I took the parchment from her hand,
And quickly read the letter there.
My memory then I did command,
To store in it this letter fair.

My Muse tried to hold back her tears,
For I started to fade away.
She whispered, "Take from me my fears,
And let not just my dreams hold sway.

For your return I now await,
And when you do we shall embrace.
Our boundless love will fully sate,
All our desires profuse apace"

Then faded I complete away,
And came awake within my bed.
I waited for the coming day,
With this dream fresh within my head.

Then, last night differently I dreamed,
That I walked on a battlefield.
It was in France, or so it seemed,
And sat a soldier by his shield.

He saw me coming close to him,
And then his head drooped toward the ground.
Exhaustion did his eye bedim.
A finished battle, I had found.

I looked around and then I saw,
The surgeons working on their wards,
To rescue them from Death's dark maw,
And wounds from axes, pikes, and swords.

I asked them where the Welshmen were,
One said, "O'er with the archer corps.
You have a strange presentment, sir.
What make you here at Agincourt?"

I said, "I also am from Wales,
And seek to find my countrymen.
I seek one who from my town hails,
To be rejoined with him again."

I walked amongst the pallets there,
Where archers Welsh did convalesce.
With stench of battle in the air,
The atmosphere did joy suppress.

I found that I was quickly drawn,
To where a group was gathered 'round.
Then with the light of breaking dawn,
I found my mark upon the ground.

He had a binding on his leg,
But still seemed apt and sound of mind.
His full attention I did beg,
And to him letter full consigned.

He started wrapped in disbelief,
But with each word, eyes wider grew.
He seemed to find a great relief,
For he knew that each word rang true.

He asked me then to say again,
The letter whole from start to end.
Emotion swept his visage then,
And asked he a reply to send.

I said for him I would commit,
To memory a message for,
And such as he think might befit,
His homebound love from Frankish war.

"I have your message full received,
By wondrous courier in a dream.
I hope it is to be believed,
And all is real, as real it seems.

I have in France received a wound,
But body mine is healing true.
I give you message finely tuned.
I promise to return to you."

Exhausted then, he fell asleep,
His body working thus to heal.
I walked away with thoughts so deep,
And questioned if this could be real.

I then awakened in my room,
And wrote the message meant for her.
I let the dream my thoughts consume,
And wondered when it next would stir.

AGINCOURT: RETURN

My dreams returned to normalcy.
A fortnight passed, as fortnights will,
But after that what do I see?
Within a dream, I'm on that hill.

So back in Wales next to the sea,
My Muse was waiting for me there.
She stood in silence next to me,
While gentle breeze stirred up her hair.

She looked at me with hopeful eyes,
And seemed as if she dared not breathe.
Emotion could not be disguised,
And underlying fear did seethe.

I felt my heart melt for my muse,
And gently touched the fairest cheek.
She could not hold. Her tears turned loose,
But soon she steeled herself to speak.

"By GOD in heaven, tell me so,
What does your visitation mean?
Have you paid that which all men owe?
Please say the purpose of this scene."

I said, "I have a missive from,
Your true love fighting down in France.
He said that he'd back to you come,
When earliest, he had the chance.

He took a wound upon the field,
But longs in Wales to come ashore.
The wound will take some time to heal,
But said he this, at Agincourt:

I have your message full received,
By wondrous courier in a dream.
I hope it is to be believed,
And all is real, as real it seems.

I have in France received a wound,
But body mine is healing true.
I give you message finely tuned.
I promise to return to you."

She grasped me in a firm embrace,
With tears of joy now flowing free.
She gasped with shock upon her face.
I turned to see what she did see.

We saw a ship at anchor there,
At Parrog out in Newport bay.
She wept, "Is this my answered prayer?
Are you back from this English fray?"

I heard soft footsteps from behind,
And turned to see a figure there.
A hooded cowl no face defined,
But figure held a regal air.

The figure spoke in dulcet voice,
As sweet to make a poet weep.
To Muse she said, "You shall rejoice.
He has returned. He's yours to keep"

My muse, with hope, left joyous dream,
The figure then turned towards the sea.
She pulled her cowl back, eyes agleam,
And 'twas my Muse looked back at me.

AGINCOURT: EPILOGUE

I did not know what I should think,
Except this is the strangest dream.
I thought I would soon from it wink,
But things are not what things might seem.

Since I could not myself awake,
I sought to see what she might say.
She smiled at me to tension break,
And said, "You should a moment stay.

I mustn't to you much reveal,
Lest cataclysmic acts ensue,
But some I need not now conceal.
You should know what I mean to you.

We are two souls bound outside time,
And living on this mortal coil,
Throughout all ages, it's sublime,
We both exist and jointly toil.

In reference mine, you're in the past,
Just as to you, her time's long gone,
But through it all our souls both last,
Regardless of how time goes on.

Reincarnation is this not,
But something else has come to be.
We've tried to understand for naught,
But we all live concurrently."

I said, "Please make me understand,
This span of many a lifetime.
How could this be, and was it planned,
That we're alive at the same time?"

She thought a bit, then answered me,
"We both seek all of what is true.
We live outside of time, you see,
And see a panoramic view.

At Pentre Ifan by the stone,
We found that something happened there.
It showed we never are alone,
But halves of an eternal pair.

Yet still we human seem to be.
Two souls that always are alive,
Thus living independently,
But throughout time together thrive.

This is quite rare that people two,
Have incarnations in each age.
With bond eternal, me and you,
Can look through time and turn each page.

Your counterpart in my own time,
Along with me through dreams can search.
We found you with your verse and rhyme.
Far in your future, we research.

We found that in the past to us,
You were the first of us to see,
And write, in faith, what we discuss,
A glimmer of all that might be.

I've always been your Oracle,
Within your writings we perceive.
It's not just metaphorical,
This inspiration you receive.

I fear I've kept you overlong,
And now release your mind to wake.
Together we are always strong,
And live we for the other's sake."

I came awake within my bed,
And felt as if a dagger's point,
Had stabbed repeatedly my head,
But thought I on this new viewpoint.

How real the dream had seemed to be,
And I could not myself awake.
I wondered if the Muse to me,
Did also this strange journey take.

Did she dream of an ancient Wales,
And see my counterpart close by,
To share with her concealed details,
And let her wake with heavy sigh?

Then I arose and took my pen,
And with it I began to write,
The details of what happened when,
My muse in dreams gave me insight.

I pondered if it could be true,
And hoped our bondage of the soul,
Is real and made me someone who,
Is one half of a greater whole.

BEING THERE

She traveled East to see the sights,
New York, with all its sounds and lights.
From there Bermuda and the beach,
For happiness within her reach.
But, as she traveled, this she thought,
That as her happiness she sought,
She wished she were beside her bear,
For she knew he'd love to be there.

Dessert at Serendipity,
Then Saks, and Lady Liberty,
Memorial to our fallen friends,
Experience all this sojourn lends.
The buildings in this wondrous place!
So beautiful St. Patrick's grace!
She thinks of these while at Times Square,
And wishes that he could be there.

Bermuda beaches, crystal seas,
With night life she true beauty sees.
She slipped into an evening dress,
And felt the garment's soft caress.
She smoothed the fabric on her hips,
A wistful smile touched her lips.
She knew that more than sights so rare,
That he would love to now be there.

As I looked in the Eastern sky,
I saw this all in my mind's eye.
She knows she means so much to me,
And I want her to happy be.
Though physically we're far apart,
That matters not to bonded heart.
For as she goes, no matter where,
She knows I always will be there.

CROSSING LINES

Society has put in place,
Lines that it bids us not to cross.
But if we do, we find disgrace,
And we can suffer massive loss.

I thought that with our timeless bond,
That we were on a different plane.
We both could show that we were fond,
With limit none, but what we deign.

But then I found there still a line,
Though not for others, only me.
And this renewed the conflict mine,
In which my worthlessness I see.

I know we both have in our minds,
To nothing do that might us end.
It rarely happens that one finds,
Eternal bond to timeless friend.

I understand we would not want,
To do things that might friendship change,
And for that reason would not flaunt,
Or something damaging arrange.

Though not because, or so I thought,
That there was no desire there,
To see what mischief could be wrought,
Between a Pixie and her bear.

This is the nature of our love,
That no conditions will be found.
For like a hand in perfect glove,
We are together gently bound.

So, though it felt like metal hot,
That cauterized a bleeding wound,
Defense for you will not be sought,
And we will stay to bond attuned.

I know you realize for my part,
I'll always seek to honor you,
And keep you safe within my heart.
I'll strive to show affection true.

So when I look around me now,
I see that what we have will last.
I care not what world will allow,
My lines to cross were long since passed.

FORGIVENESS

I made a prison in my mind,
And locked myself within.
I huddled in a corner dark,
To not get out again.

I could not answer questions that
My mind had posed to me,
And since I cannot not break these chains,
Can I ever be free?

I knew a girl while in my youth.
I treated her with love.
I told her not my feelings, though.
For I could not think of

A reason for her to love me,
Though she with me spent time.
I did not wish to pressure her,
But let her feel sublime.

She asked if I would go with her,
Upon a road trip fun.
But I was Alabama bound,
So I would miss this one.

In Hunstville, we had heard the news,
That this fair girl had died.
An accident had claimed her life.
I went outside and cried.

No more would I see her blond hair,
Nor spend my time with her.
We would not while the days away,
Her life was but a blur.

I thought and wondered if I had,
In truth treated her well.
I thought I'd done the best I could,
As far as I could tell.

I know if I had needed it,
She'd show to me her care.
Forgiving me, but when she died,
I too should have been there.

Offenses I do not store up,
I keep an empty shelf,
But although others I forgive,
I can't forgive myself.

But then one day you came to me,
And showered me with light.
Together we left prison block,
And thus ended my night.

I hope that she still smiles at me,
From GOD's home up above.
I think that I forgave myself,
Because you showed me love.

GUARDED HEART

You locked yourself within your heart,
Secure within your tower strong.
You can't be hurt while kept apart,
Though mankind misses your pure song.

We men can all be selfish things,
Desiring precious light and time,
And feeling your perfection brings.
With you our lives are made sublime.

Whether it be your touch we crave,
Or simply time with you to spend,
Did we not think of all you gave,
As we sought pleasure without end?

I ask forgiveness if I took,
For granted your light in my life.
I think I didn't, but I look,
Within my soul's eternal strife.

I see a conflict there within,
Fueled by a felt eternal bond.
Did it outside of time begin,
Millennia of feelings fond?

Perhaps you feel it differently,
And you hold all to be just dreams.
Should I have aught else let you see,
Or is all not how it all seems?

However, now, at any rate,
I'll sit outside your tower door.
I am content for you to wait,
And I'll bask in your light once more.

The selfish ones will their leave take,
For they seek only what they want.
The dark will kill them ere daybreak,
For beast of Self will them confront.

But some will be safe through the night,
As they near to your heart will stay,
And see on tower top your light,
That promises a break of day.

So, when you open tower door,
To end the rule of night's despair,
You'll notice what you sensed before,
That those who love you still are there.

HUMAN NATURE

We feel complexities in life,
And try to put them in a view,
But nature causes constant strife,
And happy times so few.

We stop and think of friends not here,
The hole they left will never fill.
Romanticism fails severe,
In a cold world that's real.

Realism paints the world in gray,
With black and white, no other hue.
We don't look forward to each day,
When we see all that's true.

So, optimism lies as such,
That everything will turn out well,
While we break everything we touch,
And hover over hell.

Now pessimism also lies,
And states that nothing good transpires.
All beauty fades and finally dies,
With all that it inspires.

All of these views are constructs of
Our intellect which helps us live.
They influence our life and love,
And how much we can give.

It does not matter, in the end,
The view we take, nor how we strive
Nor what we think our lives portend,
While we are still alive.

It seems the solace of this world,
By faith, is found in GOD's expanse,
When we in spirit form unfurled,
By death shall life enhance.

LIGHTING LIFE

There was a man lost in the dark.
He struggled on his road,
So dimly lit he could not see.
He bore a heavy load.

But then one day a brilliant light
Burst full upon the scene.
It came from someone beautiful,
An angel seldom seen.

Though human, made to offer light,
She came from up above,
And in the sky above her head,
There flew a pure white dove.

His path no longer in the dark,
He took her offered hand.
Together on the road they walked,
He now a happy man.

After some time, he thought about
The days which were a blur,
And realized that the best of times,
Were ones containing her.

She was the light unto his life.
The fuel that let him see
The beauty that surrounded him.
She made him truly free.

So, one day as they went along
She tripped upon a stone.
She hurtled toward the spiteful ground,
Which sought to break her bones.

But right before she hit the ground
She felt the strongest arms
Enfold her, catching her before
She suffered any harm.

She felt so safe when next to him,
It made emotion stir
Because she realized that he too,
Provided light for her.

And so we find that these two have
A bond beyond compare.
Eternally each other's light,
And each the other's air.

LOVE LETTERS

A woman wondered where she was,
Related to a certain man.
She only felt doubt just because,
Three words of use were under ban.

She opened up her closet door.
A vision commandeered her eyes.
For there she would her garments store,
But vision showed her their disguise.

'Twas full of garment gifts from him,
But now she saw each letters of,
The sweetest words filled to the brim.
Each one a letter full of love.

A man would sometimes doubt himself,
When thinking of this woman pure.
He felt he must desire shelf,
For he was of three words unsure.

He opened up the special chest,
In which he kept his photographs.
Each one a moment wondrous blessed,
Of life filled both with joy and laughs.

As he looked at his dearest friend,
A vision showed him truth thereof.
Each moment that she chose to spend,
With him was letter full of love.

It struck them both, as both they thought,
That three words matter not as much,
For overuse of them has wrought,
Their value less than hoped as such.

Then in their separate places they,
Both smiled as they both realized,
Love Letters aren't in what you say,
But in one's actions are disguised.

MADE OF STONE

Although I am a human man,
Most women I have ever known,
Because respect is my great plan,
Just think that I am made of stone.

I hold their feelings dear to me,
More cherished even than my own,
With me they always are carefree,
For to them, I am made of stone.

I understand that like a rock,
They see in me a strength that's shown.
Secure with me, they safely walk,
Not knowing I'm not made of stone.

In instances most rare I find,
That two souls have together grown,
And though we both are so aligned,
I must act like I'm made of stone.

So rare, in life, this deep accord.
In fact, in many, quite unknown.
The depth makes feelings stay ignored,
Perhaps I am just made of stone.

A statue in the wilderness,
Which never shall be overthrown,
But also will not feel caress,
Because it is just made of stone.

Eventually, when all things end,
I hope I will not be alone.
My parting thought to my best friend,
"Alas, I was not made of stone."

OZYMANDIUS

Am I like Ozymandius,
Whose praises all Egypt would sing?
His empire now long turned to dust,
And he is a forgotten king.

How long can memory of a man,
Outlive the span of his short life?
It seems that even with a plan,
It quickly fades from worldly strife.

Perhaps some years for most of us.
Much less for those who are alone.
In families strong it might be thus,
That he for three lifespans be known.

A thought, though, now occurs to me,
That we remember bards of old,
And if enough my writing see,
They will me in their mem'ry hold.

The end of things, to me, is sad,
For my mind ever thinks of you.
My memory in sorrow clad,
Unless you are remembered too.

So when I write you will be there,
Like Paris only Helen saw,
We still remember them and care,
And still they both our interests draw.

Perhaps we can write well enough,
That unlike an Egyptian King,
Whose memory died at time's rebuff,
Our stories might remembrance bring.

We look into the nighttime sky,
And see Orion hunting there,
He and his lover, Dawn, won't die.
Each day mankind still sees the pair.

I hope that in two thousand years,
Our writing has such love applied,
That we still help quell human fears.
If so, we will have never died.

REMEMBRANCES

Remember when you fell in love,
Upon that Summer day?
The birds came out,
And flew about,
And sang a pretty lay.

Remember when you realized,
That he would always be
Right next to you,
In all you do,
And made you two be we?

Remember when you cried at night,
When all thought he might die?
But dreams of you,
Sustained him through,
Then you again drew nigh.

Remember when you thought of him,
And how it made you smile?
A memory
Of something he,
Worked hard to make worthwhile.

Remember how he made you laugh,
At anything at all?
You both found joy,
Like a new toy,
Each day lived large and tall.

Remember how he looks at you,
And sees no other thing?
He seeks your light,
To last the night,
His angel on a wing.

Remember how each day you sought,
Each other's company?
This was a must,
Completing trust,
A bond profound and free.

Remember how you both became,
The other's need sublime?
You both now share,
Something so rare.
A love outside of time.

REMINISCING

Nostalgic, do I reminisce,
About when we together worked.
These times, admittedly, I miss.
Her pure light cleansed where darkness lurked.

I used to see her every day,
And made so many memories.
I never wished to be away,
Wanting to every moment seize.

I'd early come to work and sit,
And wait for what would soon befall.
Quite breathless waiting, I'll admit
Her high heels clicking down the hall.

I'd hear her and my breath I'd hold.
I'd stop my work and self compose,
For she whom I would soon behold,
Smiling at me in finest clothes.

Then she would burst into my view,
And fill my office with her light.
She would me with her joy suffuse.
This daily was a great delight.

She loved to dress in garments fine.
We'd photograph her to portray,
And also to a look enshrine.
We saved each Outfit Of the Day

Sometimes she would me coffee make,
And oft 'twas I that would make hers.
In Pixie cup, for goodness' sake,
A lot of cream in coffee stirs.

But in life there is constant one,
And this is that things always change.
For good or bad, for ill or fun,
We all must our lives rearrange.

In time she had to office leave.
I worried that she'd leave a hole,
Unfillable from me to reave,
The deepest bond from soul to soul.

It seems that I need not have feared,
For every day we smiles share.
There's nothing that has disappeared,
We still spend time to show we care.

Each night as I drift off to sleep,
I spare for her a bless-ed thought.
I know her in my heart I keep,
Though this was something I'd not sought.

Then every morning when I rise,
Fresh from the most enchanting dream,
I wait the opening of her eyes,
To bring me light on morning beam.

I think about the time we spend,
And how each day I seek her still.
I know our bond can never end,
So I know that I always will.

ROLES

I think that heaven sought to send,
A timeless love that has no end.
We both a lasting fire tend,
Becoming other's dearest friend

I sometimes wonder what you see,
When you take time to look at me.
Might your heart open with my key,
And might I your protector be?

Should I not give, amiss I'd feel,
All that I can for life of zeal.
I hope that I might worry seal,
Becoming a provider real.

So, did we ever enter in,
To something some consider sin?
When actions filled with love begin,
Did we not become lovers then?

Romantic poets come and go.
We write of pleasure and of woe,
But sometimes in real life we know,
That one true bond can life bestow.

SOUTHAVEN

I floated in the thickest fog,
Above a little town.
I saw the tops of buildings tall,
Afar, but not straight down.

Below I glimpsed a clearing where,
The fog had grown so thin.
So I descended to the ground,
To see what was therein.

Through soupy fog I made my way,
Upon a lakeside trail.
I was drawn to the clearing like,
A leaf before a gale.

I crossed a little bridge that spanned,
A pleasant waterfall.
I climbed some steps of stone and found,
A fenced pavilion small.

This area was free of fog,
Yet still was dimly lit.
The foggy overcast would not,
Direct sunlight admit.

Behind me then I heard a noise,
A click but nothing more.
I saw a gate of iron wrought,
That was not there before.

I noticed something passing strange,
That seemed of little use.
The sign above the gate was odd,
It read kraP NevahtouS.

I saw a bench beside the fence,
And someone sitting there,
A woman old, but beautiful,
With perfect, long white hair.

I found it odd, that though I tried,
I could not see her face.
It was as if my vision blurred,
My mem'ry to displace.

I stopped by her and said hello.
She smiled up at me.
She said "I'm happy, but surprised,
That you here I would see."

I asked her if it was the case,
That we each other knew.
She said, "It seems so long ago,
But, yes, I do know you."

She lightly patted next to her,
Inviting me to sit.
So I sat down beside her, and,
Felt pure joy, I'll admit.

She took my hand within her own,
And gave a gentle pat.
She asked me quite the question then,
As we on park bench sat.

"Did ever you feel love for me,
And hold me in your heart?
Were both our lives so intertwined,
We never were apart?"

I said "I really can't be sure,
For I can't see your face,
But if we one another knew,
Then this would be the case:

I would have showed you kindness and,
You would soon this derive,
That while I love humanity,
I've loved just women five.

So while I think you are quite nice,
The chances are, you see,
That while I showed you general love,
You were not bound to me."

She said, "Please tell me of the five,
And how you fell in love!
Was there amongst the five just one,
That seemed sent from above?"

I said, "Please, madam understand,
I value privacy,
And details of those whom I loved,
Are between them and me."

She said, "It always was your way,
To never kiss and tell.
That made trust easy for with you,
Our secrets safely dwell."

I noticed, then, she had a book,
And sought to subject change,
But when I sought the title out,
I noticed something strange.

The words within the book, it seemed,
Were backwards like the gate.
I could not read what book it was,
And asked her to relate

If she knew why within this park,
All writing was reversed?
She looked at me with liquid eyes,
And then the floodgates burst.

Through tears she said, "The reason why,
You see things as a mirror,
Is that from other side you look,
Where is no pain nor fear."

I asked her what it was she meant,
As I had not passed on.
I asked her what was happening.
Had I, then, somewhere gone?

She said, "While you were still alive,
There's no one you had left.
But finally you had to leave,
And left us all bereft.

I do not blame you, though, at all,
For you had left the way,
That all of us are forced to leave,
When GOD calls us away.

Take comfort, though, within this fact,
That ever in my need,
You always would attend to me,
And show me love by deed."

Upon my shoulder went her head.
It seemed a perfect fit.
Her white hair flowing down my chest,
I did not mind a bit.

She said, "You know, I still recall,
You told me of this place.
But until now I never thought,
That here I'd see your face."

She noticed how confused I looked,
And spoke to me again,
"This is a dream I'm having now,
Which you have entered in.

I'm dreaming of a point in time,
Wherein I lived right here.
A little town, Southaven, was
To this young woman dear.

So now, it seems, you are here too,
How you looked years ago.
Please tell me how it feels to be,
Outside time's constant flow."

I said, "I guess I did not know,
That I had passed away.
It's like I go from dream to dream,
And new things see each day."

She said, "I know you have to go,
But now before you do,
Could you make this whole place less gray,
And show a pretty view?"

I said, "This I would love to do,
But this is your fond dream.
How would I make this dream less gray,
And much more vibrant seem?"

She said, "You could just one more time,
Make up for me a poem,
And all the vibrant colors make,
So I feel like I'm home.

Perhaps you could just take some time,
And seek to tell me of,
A woman that was dear to you,
To whom you showed your love."

I said that this would be alright,
For I would not betray,
The details she would not want told,
Nor things I should not say.

So I made up a poem for her,
To make her dream be bright.
A poem about a woman dear,
Who gave me daily light:

"I do not know how long ago,
I met a woman made for me.
Not in the sense of "owning", though,
But that we fit so perfectly.

I also cannot now recall,
How many years our friendship grew,
But it is easy to recall
That what we had was something true.

For every day, I thought of her,
And wanted to spend precious time.
She made emotions in me stir,
And made my life, in short, sublime.

And every day she'd seek me out,
To simply let me know she cared.
She did not want to be without,
Me, to whom, she her soul had bared.

I sought to tell her with each day,
The gratefulness for her I felt,
And how within her light I'd stay.
She made all my defenses melt.

But others would not understand
Connection deep and so profound,
That happened when she took my hand.
Two souls forever gently bound.

She gave me light so I could see.
I showed her with her given light,
The world in all its pure beauty,
How she surpassed all things in sight.

The trees that danced with pleasant grace
To her that walked with certain sway,
Were happy to take second place.
She brought such light to ev'ry day.

The flowers clothed by GOD above,
And for her path, their petals strewn,
Bowed their sweet heads to show her love,
Romantic more than sacred moon.

Her name was whispered on the wind,
As it the trees inspired to dance.
The poets heard, and their poems penned,
And hearts were set to feel romance.

The sky seemed like a deeper blue,
The grass a perfect shade of green,
Her light showed world in beauty true,
Fueled by perfection rarely seen.

I can't recall a time before,
She was, in my life, a great part.
A woman, yes, but something more.
She made a home within my heart.

She would not like this world of gray,
Nor would she tolerate this mist,
It should disperse to light of day,
And let all be by beauty kissed.

Now everything that I can see,
Is beautiful, with no disguise,
She was the best in life to me.
I loved to look into her eyes.

I wish that I could just once more,
See her and tell her how I feel.
I miss her so and time before.
My tears cannot my sorrow heal."

I noticed while I verses made,
The scene would brighter be.
Each stanza made more flowers bloom,
And greener grass I'd see.

The woman had now gone to sleep,
Lulled by a pretty poem.
It made her dream so beautiful.
I hoped she felt at home.

My tears had started now to flow,
Based on the memory,
Of my best friend so beautiful,
And what she meant to me.

As one tear finally hit the ground,
The fog all disappeared.
We both surrounded by great light,
All darkness now had cleared.

I sought, then from her dream to go
And leave her sitting there.
I gently moved my shoulder out,
From under soft blond hair.

I tried to loosen hold she had,
And let go of her hand.
Her grip just tightened when I tried.
I did not understand.

I softly whispered to her, "Please,
I must leave dream I'm in."
She whispered back through full soft lips,
"I'll not let go again."

I realized then, just who she was,
For she could not disguise.
She smiled as she showed to me,
Her beautiful green eyes.

No longer was she elderly,
But as she was before.
I clearly now saw who she was:
She whom my heart was for.

She said, "You finally recognized,
The woman that you knew.
I'm tired of just sitting here,
I think I'll leave with you!"

So she got up, and hand in hand,
We started both to walk.
We had some catching up to do,
So also did we talk.

We left by way of Iron gate,
No longer in the dark.
The sign above now wholly changed.
It said, "Southaven Park".

Edward Bowman

THE CELL

I sit within my prison cell,
A grated window far above.
Most light cannot reach where I dwell,
And my thoughts turn to whom I love.

I wonder how this came to be,
While fighting back the welling tears,
I crave the light so I can see,
And thus defeat my grief and fears.

How is it I sit in the dark,
Chained to these walls of coldest stone?
Should I still hope in setting stark,
That I'll not always be alone?

As tears well over, do I think,
Of bond with her so strong and fair.
The tears away I try to blink,
But teeter on most black despair.

The bond has never faltered ere,
And I still feel her presence there.
I focus on our memories dear,
And bring emotion strong to bear.

I feel her through our mystic link.
She seems to be so close to me.
Despair now flees for now I think,
That I soon now with her shall be.

Through window high, I see a glow,
And hear soft footsteps in the night.
I smile, then, for now I know,
That she will give to me her light.

THE TWO WOLVES

The wolves that live out in the wild,
In elegant society,
Have loves so great in them compiled,
They live without anxiety.

They love the freedom of their kind,
To roam the steppes and mountain's pass.
And in their hunt, they are refined.
They will not past their need harass.

They love the way that they fit in,
To be with those wolves that they love.
They live without a thought of sin,
As was designed by GOD above.

Complexity within them reigns.
They live with Order, but live free.
Perfection in this life remains,
A lesson in all we could be.

I now look at the inner me,
And see a wolfish manner true.
'Tis you who finally made me see,
The wolves that are both me and you.

Edward Bowman

TRANSPORT

I'm not sure when it was I died,
For she was there and though she cried,
I could see nothing else but her,
Though tears did both our visions blur.

Her perfect beauty made me sigh,
For she the apple of my eye,
Made all things better in my life,
And always lifted me from strife.

I looked into her limpid eyes,
And saw in them Celestial Skies.
I smelled the scent upon her hair,
Always so lovely and so fair.

I felt her touch upon my hand,
So soft and gentle, yet so grand.
She lightly kissed my pallid brow.
My failing heart leapt up and how.

All things about her I could feel,
Were in a single word, ideal.
I sailed to heaven up above,
On waves of her exquisite love.

I noticed there the pearl wrought gates,
The best of either of man's fates.
I entered to eternal light,
Where is no sorrow nor no night.

I thought about her left behind.
An idea formed within my mind:
That though I now walked streets of air,
With her I was already there.

VALKYRIE

Did you not look at me with love,
While I fought on the raging sea?
And while the battle round me raged,
Did thoughts of you not comfort me?

Did you not look at me with love,
While I fought bravely in the air?
And did you while my craft crashed down,
Give solace by your tender care?

Did you not look at me with love,
While I fought in a foreign land?
And did you notice every drop,
Of blood I spilled upon the sand?

Have you now come to me with love,
To take me from this brutal flame?
As I know I cannot survive,
With my last breath, I say your name.

...

At last I come to you in love,
For you have always thought of me.
You know as now I take you home,
I'll always be your Valkyrie.

WALKS OF LIFE

I walked with Hatred in my life,
But she was very mean.
She made me presents of great strife,
And speech that was obscene.

With Sorrow, then, I walked a while.
She never said a word.
She never wanted me to smile,
And with tears my eyes blurred

So then I walked with Apathy,
But never did she care.
She thought indifference made her free,
But this life one can't share.

And then fulfilled from up above,
I walked with someone new.
It seems I never walked in love,
Until I walked with you.

DIVISION III: THE LIGHT THAT ALL MEN SEEK

THE GLORY FOUND IN THE LIGHT OF LOVING

AND BEING LOVED IN RETURN

A KISS

Would it be such a sin to kiss,
The woman that you love,
To be enrapt in purest bliss,
And ride the wave thereof?

For in that moment, time would stop,
Eternity therein.
You'd soar above the mountain top,
And feel something begin.

You'd feel her melt into your chest,
Two hearts that beat as one,
And in this timeless moment's crest,
All else becomes as none.

For timeless now, and time before,
Your universe contained,
Within this woman you adore,
And just to her constrained.

You'll feel her breath as your lips part,
So gentle on your cheek.
She's made her home within your heart,
Fulfilling all you seek.

You look into her liquid eyes,
And seek therein to drown.
Submerging into her the prize,
Her love your life's true crown.

You'll touch her hair and hold her close,
To keep her safe from harm.
She will affection yours engross,
By touch upon your arm.

Her head upon your shoulder laid,
Your life is perfect now.
She answered all for which you prayed,
And all life could allow.

A LETTER TO YOUR MOTHER

Dear mother of my dearest friend,
I thought that I would write,
To you the briefest note of thanks,
For bringing forth such light.

The other day we sat and talked,
A pleasant time indeed.
You must know that your progeny,
Does ev'ry dream exceed.

I know that life is so complex,
With naught in vacuum made.
I know that for perfection found,
A key role you have played.

No matter what it is I feel,
It cannot be denied,
You are part of who she is,
And her support supplied.

Although, in all ways perfect she
Three things enter my mind,
Her beauty , strength and intellect,
Perfectly intertwined.

Her beauty fueled by inner light,
Shall never pass away.
It's carried in her ancient soul,
Increasing ev'ry day.

Her strength cannot be overcome,
So great to seem unreal.
She brings to mind the picture of,
A rose made out of steel.

While her great beauty first attracts,
The eye of every man,
Her tow'ring intellect will keep,
Them 'round her as they can.

For my part, maybe you should know,
We share the strongest bond.
I always will be there for her.
It seems, of her, I'm fond.

So, let me once more give my thanks,
To you who from her birth,
Helped shape her into who she is:
Perfection found on Earth.

A WHISPER

I heard a whisper in the air,
It spoke of flowing golden hair,
And softest lips surrounding smile.
I stopped to listen for a while.

I closed my eyes and listened then,
To what seems like it's always been,
A gentle voice describing friend,
And carried on the sweetest wind.

I felt a hand take hold of mine,
And destiny two souls align.
I felt her standing next to me,
And wondered if she just might be

As beautiful as in my mind,
And if in her, perchance, I'd find
A kindred soul to share my path,
And confidant to dispel wrath.

A short prayer thrown into the skies,
And then I opened up my eyes.
What I saw then made hot tears fall,
For she had no defect at all.

A perfect woman dressed in black,
My jaw must have gone fully slack.
She devastated me in kind,
Surpassing image in my mind.

Her eyes held mine, and called me in
To swim in pools both pure and twin.
I never wish to take my leave,
But rather to her presence cleave.

So now she's never far away,
And we spend time most every day.
When we cannot with friend most fond,
Be present still we feel the bond.

I sometimes sit upon the hill,
Beside the gently flowing rill,
And still the breeze with gentle mien,
Whispers the name of Novalene.

Edward Bowman

AFTERIMAGE

Lost in thought, unto the sun,
I turned my pensive gaze.
The brilliant light destroyed my sight,
Yet warmed me with its rays.

With wat'ring eyes I turned away,
And noticed I now saw,
A purple afterimage of the
Sun I held in awe.

For moments there was naught I saw
Except for purple spot.
It dominated all my sight,
And other vision fought.

I found in this the truth about,
Just what you mean to me.
I wish that there were words to say,
So you'd know what I see.

The first time I laid eyes on you,
I looked upon your face.
You filled my senses and my dreams.
I bask within your grace.

I gazed into your blinding light,
And knew we'd never part.
Your soul an afterimage burned
Directly on my heart.

Profound it is, this bond we share.
Its gentle, strong and true.
And now, no matter where I go,
My eyes see only you.

APART

From you who occupies my mind,
I do not wish to be apart.
I close my eyes and there I find,
That you, indeed, have filled my heart.

I told you in another poem,
And, hopefully, you know its true,
No matter where we both might roam,
Where e'er I am I carry you.

So if, perchance, you feel the need,
And miss me being close nearby,
We can commune should you take heed.
Just go out and look to the sky.

If it is during light of day,
Just turn and face the warming sun.
I will be there upon a ray,
And you will know we still are one.

But better still the sacred night,
Where you can see the northern star,
Or gaze at moon's romantic light,
And know that we together are.

For every day the sun I'll see
And every night the stars and moon.
You'll know you're not apart from me.
I will return and see you soon.

ARRIVAL

I did not know how dark it was,
For light was taken bit by bit.
Romantic soul suppressed because,
My point of view could never fit

With expectations set on me,
And chains of Iron weighing down.
My strength can calm a raging sea,
But still I'm paid with just a frown.

Sometimes it makes me worthless feel,
For needed, but not wanted, I.
I wonder is this feeling real?
Will I be wanted ere I die?

I sat within a darkened room,
Alone except for pain and grief.
But then I smelled a sweet perfume,
And trembled I, as if a leaf.

You came and stood beside my chair,
And gently touched my outstretched hand.
I stood and touched your golden hair,
And suddenly a flame was fanned.

I looked into your perfect eyes,
And felt a closeness so profound.
Did you come down from heaven's skies,
And are you to me gently bound?

My world was then refilled with light.
And now, it seems, I clearly see.
You have dispelled eternal night,
For you want to spend time with me.

And for my part, I can't repay
How beautiful you made my view.
I look now forward to each day,
And now my eyes see only you.

BLINDED

I feel a warmth within my life,
A gift from special one.
I bask within her heat and light,
As if she were the sun.

(I give to him the warmth he feels
And need no recompense.
He always seeks to be with me,
And puts up no defense.)

I want more time within her light,
Because I do not feel,
The same when night time comes around,
For she my soul doth heal.

(Each morning when I come awake,
I know that he'll be there.
Each night he holds his breath for me,
And with my light takes air.)

One day, I turned my face upon
Her light within my skies.
I felt her gaze upon my face,
And opened up my eyes.

(I'm close to this most grateful man,
For mine's the biggest part,
Of space that he in fondness keeps,
For those in his great heart)

Too beautiful for human eyes,
I forfeited my sight.
My eyes within their sockets burned.
I'm blinded by her light.

(One day when I could not contain,
The scale of my fair grace.
He opened up his eyes to me.
My light caressed his face.)

So, now it is I see naught else,
Of life I've left behind,
But live in joy because she deemed
Me worthy man to blind.

(So now we both the bonds of light
Shall never leave behind.
We happy both because I found
My worthy man to blind.)

COMPLETED DAY

My day was very full today,
Though not unusual to see.
With all that life might send my way,
I am a very busy bee!

From my arising with the sun,
Until the sandman visits me,
There's always something to be done,
And things to which just I can see.

With all that said, I noticed this,
A feeling that my day's not done.
I wonder what might be amiss,
My day not finished, though 'twas fun.

But then I see a wondrous light,
And feel again a presence sweet.
You visit me, a bless-ed sight,
At last my day is now complete.

DISCOVERY

I did not think it could occur,
That I should find someone like her.
Perfection found upon the Earth,
This woman of infinite worth.

Only with her does all feel right.
I bask within her precious light.
She holds me with soft eyes of green,
More beautiful than ever seen.

I wonder, could it ever be,
That when apart she misses me?
I'm grateful if she understands,
I put my heart within her hands.

Edward Bowman

DO YOU MISS ME YET

I often miss my dearest friend,
Who to my life the Lord did send.
Upon her light I now depend.
I know our bond will never end.

I don't prefer to be apart
From she who woke my dormant art.
I realize now, 'twas from the start
She had her place within my heart.

DO YOU REALIZE

Today you wore a purple shirt,
Completed with the checkered skirt,
Emblazoned in my memory,
How beautiful you are to me,
With elegance overt.

As I helped you out of the car,
I knew I was most blessed by far
By your consent to moments spend,
With me. I wish they would not end,
Fulfilling as they are.

I don't think there could ever be,
A woman I more need to see.
I blink the tears back from my eyes,
And don't think that you realize
Just what you mean to me.

DOUBT

I doubted that I ever would,
Discover something found by few.
I never knew there even could,
Be someone on the Earth like you.

I doubted that you'd draw me close,
But found that we already were.
As if a drug, your daily dose,
Emotions deep within me stir.

I doubt that we might ever know,
The depth of bond that we have found,
I'll shelter you when storm winds blow,
For gladly, I am to you bound.

So, should you ever come to doubt
That there is love condition free,
Or happiness seems blotted out,
Extend your hand, and reach for me.

EACH TIME

Each time, it seems, I close my eyes,
I find that you are also there.
I feel where your sweet soul now lies,
And smell the scent of flaxen hair.

Each time my eyes I open up,
Fantastic colors frame my sight.
Great beauty fills my battered cup.
You fill me once again with light.

Each time my heart beats in my chest,
My lifeblood flows with power new.
Each pair of pulsing, then of rest,
Marks out the time 'til I'm with you.

Each time my heart will skip a beat,
The cause is not beyond my ken.
Each time it skips, I'm made complete,
Because I've just seen you again.

Each time my breath is wholly lost,
Away it's taken by a queen.
In tears, but happy, I am lost,
Within the greatest beauty seen.

Each time my breath has been regained,
I know I'm favored amongst men.
With fondness that cannot be feigned,
I am fulfilled to breathe you in.

Edward Bowman

ENCOUNTER

She looked at him without surprise,
As he fell in her lovely eyes.
He could not breathe. There was no air.
He gently touched the softest hair.

She smiled and sighed at his fond touch,
Because she knew it meant so much.
She made his feelings all astir,
His universe contained in her.

Her skin seemed to him also soft,
While perfumed air from her did waft.
He held her close, and thought that he
Might not a better moment see.

In all his life he did not know,
That he could be affected so.
He closed his eyes and dreamed his dreams,
And felt a profound bond it seems.

A gentle chain upon his heart,
Awareness of her now a part,
Of life now full of light and grace,
Because of her tender embrace.

Not just the physical, of course,
Created bond nor was the source.
The spirits two, it seems to me,
A perfect fit eternally.

ENOUGH FOR ME

I've seen great beauty in my life,
And, yet, I seek it still.
Though some might think I've seen enough,
And that I've had my fill.

Although I've roses seen before,
I still want to see them.
How beautiful the petals soft,
And thorns upon the stem.

The moon I've seen above me in
The still and sacred night.
Yet never would I tire of,
Its soft romantic light.

I oftentimes have stood and watched,
The beauty of the trees,
But still I want to see them dance,
And whisper in the breeze.

In Winter I have felt the snow,
Fall gently on my face.
Yet, still, I want to see and feel,
This sign of Winter's grace.

How oft have I took in the air,
Fresh after storm in Spring?
But still I love that freshest scent,
That makes me want to sing.

And though I've seen you oft before,
I know it will not be,
That seeing you just one more time,
Will be enough for me.

Edward Bowman

EVENING PRAYER

As I now lay me down to sleep.
I pray the LORD my soul to keep.
I notice as I count the sheep,
It seems I cannot help but weep.

My tears of joy my sorrows drowned,
For I've the truest beauty found.
Amazing to be gently bound,
And happiness does now abound.

She both my heart and feelings stir,
With smallest thought of time with her.
The many years seem like a blur,
But each day brand new things occur.

I pray that there is no mistake,
For this would serve my heart to break.
If I am dreaming, for my sake,
I pray that I do not awake.

EVERYTHING

I see your grace in swaying trees.
I see your soul in perfect skies.
I feel your touch upon the breeze.
In woodland pools I see your eyes.

I sense you in the sacred night,
The strongest bond from soul to soul,
The stars and moon with gentle light,
Remind me that you make me whole.

I hear your voice in forest brook.
I close my eyes and feel your hair.
I do not even have to look,
But sense it in the softest air.

A rose bows to your perfect lips,
For color and their softness too.
I then remember lovely hips,
In gentle slope of hill I view.

I feel your warmth within the sun.
A smile on my upturned face.
Though others try, you are the one,
That occupies my heart with grace.

To summarize, I realize now,
You are in all I feel and see.
This evidence makes me avow,
That you are everything to me.

FAIR WINDS

My Pixie soon will go away,
And bless Orlando with her light.
She brings to all Dawn's glorious ray,
And shatters chains made by the night.

I think that I my breath shall hold,
With maybe one last gasp of air:
A picture of her grace enrolled,
With purest eyes, and softest hair.

I wonder if it is OK,
As my emotions deeply stir,
To let her know when she's away,
That I will always think of her.

FEELINGS

I sometimes don't know how to say,
How feelings for you might have grown.
With you, I want to spend each day.
You never have to be alone.

As our bond has become profound,
You have become my source of light.
How pleasant is it to be bound,
To someone who dispels the night.

I find that tears spring when I think,
Of how close that you are to me,
How perfect is our gentle link,
And how fulfilling this can be.

I turn my face up to the skies,
And know that GOD has smiled at me,
For every time I close my eyes,
It's only you I always see.

FONDNESS

A fondness strong between them grew,
Though how and why, neither quite knew.
So quickly bound with bond so true,
With deepest love, the gentle glue.

Each time he sought to think of her,
Emotion deeply felt would stir
He felt as if he sweetly were,
A part of something good and pure.

Each time her thoughts would turn to him,
Especially with life stressed and grim.
She would in his devotion swim,
And knew their light would never dim,

They found that soon they occupied,
Their thoughts and dreams. They could not hide
The truth that always will abide,
Each better by the other's side.

GIFTS

She asked if she might have the moon.
I thought I would comply.
I lassoed it and gave to her,
The full moon from our sky.

She thought the sun might be a gift,
A bauble she could wear.
I gathered it into a gem,
So she would know I care.

I thought of what else I could give,
To show her this bond ours.
With happiness I wrapped them up,
And gave to her the stars.

Edward Bowman

GIVING THE TIME OF DAY

When in the morning I awake,
I wait upon your light.
It lets me see the path ahead,
After the dark of night.

Mid morning, I sit at my desk,
And think about you there.
I see your beauty in my mind,
And feel the softest hair.

Throughout the morning, we have talked,
And now we come to noon.
I share with you my earnest hope,
That I might see you soon.

In afternoon, I stop to think,
About the place you hold,
Within my heart. I know you are
More valuable than gold.

The evening comes, I find that we,
The hours wile away.
We share together fun and dreams,
Until we end the day.

When night arrives, I tuck you in,
As gentle as it seems.
Then take my rest and find that I,
Still see you in my dreams.

While I'm asleep, I have no doubt,
A smile's on my face.
For soon a day will start again,
And I'll bask in your grace.

When I think on which times of day,
I sense your bond with me.
I realize that I always feel,
How much you mean to me.

HELD

Are you not held in God's great grace,
Which fuels your glow of inner light?
Your spirit in a perfect vase,
I look thereon and end my night.

Are you not held within my sight?
To you I turn my tired eye.
For you I scale the utmost height,
You take my hand and pull me nigh.

Are you not held within my hand?
I have no need to seek control.
Emotion by perfection fanned,
For deep connection makes us whole.

Are you not held within my heart,
Enthroned in gilded chamber there?
When was it that we chose to start
To show each other that we care?

Are you not held in high esteem,
The tallest pedestal of all?
I promise, though, oh morning beam,
That I will never let you fall.

Am I not held in some regard,
By she who holds such gentle sway?
The care I have for her unmarred,
I try to show her every day.

HER YARD

I stood outside the picket fence,
With all the other boys.
They clamored at the fastened gate,
And made an awful noise.

Some tried to open gate by force,
With no shame others lied,
And all received a fate the same:
They all were kept outside.

I looked over the sturdy gate,
To see what might be there.
T'was then I first laid eyes on her;
She with the flaxen hair.

She looked at me with purest eyes,
Two pools of sacred green.
A holy light poured from her frame;
A beauty seldom seen.

Two crystal tears formed in her eyes,
And drifted down her cheek.
Compassion stirred within my heart.
I sought with her to speak.

She said, "You are no different than
The other men outside.
You seek me for your pleasure, so
You seek to be inside."

I said, "You are correct in that
I'm just like any man.
I'm subject to my nature, but
I do the best I can

To keep myself under control,
And chain the beast within.
I'd cherish you for who you are,
but not in how we'd sin."

So, then I came back every day,
And talked to her at length.
I tried to show her deference,
And she lent me her strength.

One day I looked around me, and
Became more grateful bard.
While other boys still clamored, she
Had let me in her yard.

HOW BEAUTIFUL

How beautiful the sun that gives,
Its warmth to all upon the Earth.
Sustaining life to all that lives,
One cannot overstate its worth.

How beautiful is the fair moon,
That gives to us a gentler light.
Its Aegis is a special boon,
That guides two lovers in the night.

How beautiful the distant stars,
So constant in their stately dance.
They sailors guide 'cross oceans ours,
And with the moon inspire romance.

How beautiful the stately trees.
With elegance so pure and rare.
With grace they sway within the breeze,
And give to us our needed air.

As beautiful as all these are,
All made by GOD who dwells above.
One thing might their great beauty mar,
That none are capable of love.

Although these all great beauty show,
Another made by GOD I see.
Made perfectly, and did you know,
How beautiful you are to me?

Edward Bowman

HOW WE ARE

I'm glad that it has come to be,
That when I close my eyes I see,
Your beauty and your light so free.
I know you're always there with me.

I think you might have noticed, too,
A fact that always will be true.
No matter what you're going through,
I always will be there with you.

We seem connected at the core,
We cherish each and both adore.
Our spirits now to such heights soar,
Can we remember time before?

IF LOVE WERE

If love were like a gentle rain,
I'd be soaked through and through,
Because I seek no shelter from,
This cyclone caused by you.

If love were but the lightest breeze,
I'd dwell up in the sky.
My feet could never touch the ground.
Such wind would make me fly.

If love were like a candle in,
The darkness of the night.
I'd have to squint my eyes against,
The brilliance of the light.

If love were but a single thread,
So warm would I be kept.
Wrapped up within the thickest cloth,
No cold would it accept.

If love were like the smallest flame,
I'd be consumed in fire.
But happy in inferno's rage,
I'd stay upon the pyre.

If love were indescribable
My dreams might have come true.
For I cannot express, it seems,
How I'm fulfilled by you.

JUST A MAN

Was even there a time before
The two of us began?
I find I can't remember such,
Although, I'm just a man.

We are, it seems, both gently bound,
According to a plan.
A bond I think I don't deserve,
For I am just a man.

This bond, exquisite, joins me with,
For more than one lifespan,
A perfect woman made of light,
Though I am just a man.

Society with coldest heart,
This kind of love might ban.
I cannot want this bond to break,
For I am just a man.

Most days I fight with my desire,
For I know you're more than,
An object for one's carnal needs,
But still, I'm just a man.

I try to treat you as I should,
With true love at the van,
I wish that I could better be.
Alas, I'm just a man.

With no conditions in our hearts,
We love as best we can.
You're like an angel sent from heav'n,
While I am just a man.

One day I'll go to my reward,
When my life's had its span.
I hope you'll feel to you I was,
Much more than just a man.

LIGHTNING STRIKE

'Twas on a day with cloudless skies,
That lightning struck me where I stood.
My last thought was of your green eyes,
And that I hoped you understood

How much I really care for you.
You fill my thoughts both night and day.
I wondered if you really knew.
It's so much more than I can say.

The lightning hit me on my cheek,
And instantly my body tensed.
The heavy charge began to seek,
All nerves throughout my body sensed.

Each nerve made wonderfully aware,
Of new sensations all around.
An ecstacy beyond compare,
Within this lightning strike was found.

My eyes were filled with sacred light.
So happy was I to be blind.
My senses gave me second sight,
My mortal body left behind.

It must have just a moment been,
But seemed like an eternity.
I tried to take a breath again,
Completely filled with energy.

Ironic, now, how at the end,
I feel like I am filled with life,
My focus is on you, my friend,
And you have calmed my deepest strife.

I noticed then, I had not died,
My sight returned, I now could see.
When I saw truth I almost cried,
For this was just you touching me.

Edward Bowman

LIVING WHILE ALIVE

I noticed that you cried
Upon the day I died.
Was it for my departure that you wept?
Don't cry, my dearest friend.
Our bond can never end,
For we each in the other's heart are kept.

Remember our bound lives.
A new day now arrives,
When I must be held in fond memory
You must wait for the day
When veil is torn away
And once again together we will be.

And did we ever sin?
Perhaps some now and then,
But we together through our lives did strive.
With all the time we spent
And places that we went
We chose to really live while still alive.

LOOKING THROUGH MY EYES

I wish that you could use my eyes,
To look upon yourself.
You'd see a beauty so profound,
You could not feelings shelf.

I wish that you could use my eyes,
To look upon your form.
You'd see the perfect female curves,
That makes reaction warm.

I wish that you could use my eyes,
To see your lovely hair.
You'd think that it would feel so soft,
As if 'twere made of air.

I wish that you could use my eyes,
To look into your own.
You want to just fall in them both,
And sink just like a stone.

I wish that you could use my eyes,
To see you as I do.
You'd find a woman made of light,
And see the perfect you.

LUNCH WITH MY MUSE

I sat across from her at lunch.
My heart jumped in my chest.
Her beauty cannot be defined.
Amongst men I am blessed.

At lunch the moments quickly passed.
Too soon we had to part.
Though sad, I take great comfort in
Her place within my heart.

As I helped her into her car,
I looked into her eyes.
I saw in them the beauty that
Reflects the crystal skies.

Back at the shop, whilst at my desk,
She sent a pic of her.
Beholding perfect woman there,
Emotions were astir.

I always miss her very soon,
After we go our ways.
I feel like something's missing, and
I'd rather that she stays.

She mentioned just the other day,
What all gifts mean to her.
They bear her fond remembrance and
Some raw emotions stir.

A man that shows her this regard,
To tell her with a gift,
The way he needs her in his life,
Gives her a special lift.

She sees him when she sees herself
Whilst looking in the mirror.
Her lips are touched by briefest smile.
She wishes he were here.

I wish that every day she could,
See something I her gave.
Then she might each day think of me,
And on her heart engrave

Some memory in fondness held,
Of when we spent some time,
Or maybe something general.
A bond that is sublime.

I wondered then, what could transpire
To make things the reverse.
What catalyst could make her seem
To be my universe?

What would make me carry each day,
In thought, this beauty true?
It must be something in the past,
'Cause I already do.

Edward Bowman

MAGNETISM

In nature, magnets, if aligned,
Pull on each other with such force,
It seems they want to be combined,
If living things they were, of course.

The nature of attraction strong,
In metals magnetized, you see,
Will dissipate with distance long,
And will attract the next they see.

The magnetism of our bond,
Which has the both of us combined,
Compels in us the feelings fond,
But is made from two souls aligned.

The differences to metal pull,
Of which I know at least of two,
Make the distinction vast and full,
From magnets that are me and you.

The first concerns what's in between,
Since this won't change and never will.
The greater distances just mean,
That our bond will grow stronger still.

The second part, which means much more,
Is metals will demagnetize,
But our eternal bond will soar
And will not suffer time's demise.

Should all around us turn to dust,
You'll always be my premier care.
No distance should forestall your trust,
That I will constantly be there.

MONTHLY REMEMBRANCE

Deep snow lays silent on the ground,
A silent blanket all around.
So January, with year new,
Brings also pristine beauty true.

Odd how the snow in beauty lays,
And brings to me joy everyday,
But this just makes me think on her,
And in me something deeply stir.

Now February comes around
And still the snow is on the ground.
We breathlessly await a thaw.
Still Winter's beauty has no flaw.

Though beautiful the Winter scene,
My thoughts are still on Novalene.
The landscape just cannot compete,
Because her beauty is complete.

Finally, March brings warmer climes.
Reminding of us of lovely times.
The snow is melted. Spring is here.
The time of rebirth now is near.

Old dance of seasons carries on,
And Winter now has finally gone,
But more alluring than the Spring,
Is she whose beauty makes hearts sing.

Roughly does April now descend.
With storms that turbulence portend.
The sky filled with fantastic light,
And thunder pealing through the night.

Edward Bowman

Great beauty in ferocious storms
Is one of April's telltale norms,
But tempest's beauty in the skies
Is not as pretty as her eyes.

Elated now that May is here,
And flowers blooming now this year,
I see bright colors everywhere,
The beauty all around so fair.

Though everywhere the flowers are,
And nothing can their beauty mar,
They bow their petals in their place
When she walks by with perfect grace.

Months go by fast and June is here.
The warmth makes sadness disappear.
We bask within the glorious rays
The Sun provides these Summer days

E'en though I love the radiant sun
That metes out life to everyone,
I'd rather feel her energy,
For it seems she brings life to me.

Yet even in July we find,
A heat that no one seems to mind.
June's warmth has turned to blazing heat
And gives us reason all to meet

On certain days at swimming pools,
Where water both us soothes and cools.
E'en so she still the pools defy
With limpid pools that are her eyes.

Unless we yearn for colder days,
We revel in the August haze.
The stifling heat the Summer's bid,
To last until the Fall forbid.

Resplendent beauty in clear skies,
With graceful land combines and vies
With anything that has allure,
But still cannot compete with her.

E'en as September cools the air,
And for the Fall the trees prepare.
Their leaves in hues of orange and red,
The trees make ready them to shed

My eyes well up at such a sight,
Of rustic beauty of leaves' plight,
And as the winds through branches stir,
The leaves, like all, will fall for her.

Yet in October, Fall's in force.
The days, due to the seasons' course,
Grow shorter, and more time is spent
By fireside with book content.

Let us look into dancing flames,
Which our imagination claims.
Fantastic dancers most sublime,
It is for her they're marking time.

In coldest rain November comes,
And loudly on the rooftop drums.
We take the time to give our thanks.
The harvest's in, our glasses raise.

Gold sheaves adorn the beauteous field.
I walk among the farmer's yield.
The stacks are soft and yellow there,
But pale before her lovely hair.

Has old December finally come,
So Earth can to it's spell succumb?
In beauty does all nature sleep,
And covered with a blanket deep.

Though all the months with life abound,
And beauty throughout all is found,
More beautiful than all is she.
It seems she means the world to me.

MY EYES

I always find you beautiful,
And try to tell you every day.
It's not just being dutiful,
But it is something I should say.

I said it once to make a point,
Because you had not done your hair.
You worried that you'd disappoint,
I did not want you to despair.

I smiled and said, "I wish that you,
Could see yourself, but with my eyes.
You'd be convinced of beauty true,
And all the grace that with you lies."

You smiled back and knew that I,
Would always see your beauty there.
However, you did not know why,
Or how we made this bond we share.

We talked a while, and then I left,
Our evenings physically apart.
We later talked. We're not bereft,
Because we're in each other's heart.

Then later, we both went to sleep,
And something happened, most extreme.
In slumber both profound and deep,
We entered someone else's dream.

We stand together in a den,
With sunlit windows warming air,
We hear a quiet bell, and then,
An oracle confronts us there.

The hooded figure turns to me,
And bids me on a chair recline.
She said, "Through your eyes she shall see,
If you to her your sight consign."

I nod, and laying further back,
In comfort, notice coming sleep.
The oracle, dressed all in black,
Engages you with idea deep.

"You now have his express consent,
To see how he all things would view.
However, we need your assent,
Before we lend his sight to you.

Before you do, we must declare,
That you will gain more than his sight.
While he sleeps blind upon that chair,
You'll feel, too, his emotions' might."

You smile and say that you would like,
To feel and witness what I see.
The oracle, almost ghostlike,
Bids you to stand right next to me.

With her right hand below my brow,
And her left hand with you the same,
She covers both our eyes, and now,
She let's you all my senses claim.

I drift down into conscious sleep,
Where I still notice every thing,
But yet in dream so strong and deep,
To you all my sensations wing.

The oracle then pats my cheek.
She gently smiles down at me,
Then gives to you a gift unique.
And with my eyes, you now can see.

Before she moves her mystic hand,
You notice, first, your sense of smell.
Refined, although you had not planned,
For scent to such a story tell.

The open windows let the air,
With flowered scent into the den.
It carries fragrance of your hair,
Which makes you feel in love again.

Emotions rising due to this,
You hear upon the gentle breeze,
A song of ancient love and bliss,
That's softly sung by swaying trees.

The oracle yet blocks your sight,
Still covering your new found eyes.
She then suggests a touch so light,
To see what feeling might arise.

You lightly touch your radiant face,
And then you stroke your lovely hair.
Your soft skin makes your heart to race,
And tresses like caressing air.

With breeze now whispering your name,
The oracle now takes your hand.
She faces you to window's frame,
And frees your eyes to vision grand.

You notice all the colors first,
The grass so green and sky so blue,
All things in sight profoundly burst,
With beauty colorful and true.

You think you spot a unicorn,
That frolics on a distant hill.
A wizard by a Gryphon borne,
Flies by and gives you quite a thrill.

You spend an hour at the pane,
As landscape shifts from scene to scene.
Each beautiful and without stain,
Your heart now leaps for what you've seen.

Emotions rise as you now know,
The poet is the artist who,
Sees beauty everywhere although,
The light so he can see is you.

The oracle now gently turns,
You 'round to face a full length mirror,
Your curiosity now burns,
Though while you turn you fight down fear.

You know not why you are afraid,
To see the truth of what he sees,
You know he finds you perfect made,
And always puts you at your ease.

You look at your reflection there,
And start to cry, but not from fright.
You weep for from your toes to hair,
You see a woman made of light.

Through happy tears you see your form,
So feminine with perfect curves,
You feel desire start to warm,
With heightened senses in your nerves.

Your eyes look now upon your face,
The tears start flowing even more,
For all you see is purest grace,
More beautiful than e'er before.

You see your lips, so soft and pink,
That put to shame the fairest rose.
Their fullness causes you to think,
That they could paradise impose.

At last you look into your eyes,
Emotion sends you to your knees.
You cannot stop the tears that rise,
And flow because of what he sees.

You see two limpid pools of green,
And through them, too, the purest soul.
You're moved by such perfection seen,
And feel like half of greater whole.

You hardly can withstand the sight,
Of thorough beauty from above,
Or woman fashioned from the light.
You feel the bond of endless love.

With blinding tears you turn to see,
The oracle still standing there.
She asks you to stand next to me,
Where I sit sleeping in the chair.

In fondness do you touch my cheek,
My sight gently returns to me,
I start to wake, but feel so weak,
But I know why this had to be.

The oracle just smiles at us.
She seems to know what we have found.
That since we have made choices thus,
We are together gently bound.

Then once again we hear the bell,
The oracle then takes her leave,
She smiles and says, "All now is well,
But I must now this dream unweave".

We know it's time to leave the dream.
We all begin to fade from sight,
And you now know you're what you seem:
Perfection fashioned from the light.

MY FORTUNE

I know I have been blessed in life.
In comfort do I live.
My resources right now exceed,
All that I wish to give.

I wonder at the grace of GOD,
My treasure does abound,
But when I stop to think on it,
Is this my pleasure found?

I thought about a circumstance,
Should my resources fall.
I found out that to my surprise,
I wouldn't mind at all.

In life our riches come and go,
Prescribed by GOD above,
Far more important people are,
And demonstrating love.

I guess I've known this most my life,
But now it's proven true.
For I DO have a fortune, and,
My fortune's found in you.

Edward Bowman

NEED

There is a woman who I know,
Who's perfect as can be.
It seems I am most fond of her,
And she seems fond of me.

Each day we realize more and more,
There's no space in between,
The way that we're together put,
A bond strong, but unseen.

Our days do not now seem complete,
If we don't spend some time,
To make each other smile, and,
To fuel a flame sublime.

She brings with her, where e'er she goes,
A pure and perfect light.
She filled me to the brim with it,
And ended my long night.

This made such feeling in me rise,
A wonderful thing rare.
She knows that I love our sweet bond,
And always will be there.

I have to fight my baser thoughts,
Because I am a man.
They are not based in shallow lust,
And I cannot them ban.

But then I think about her needs,
My own to side are shoved,
And try to show her love the way,
That she needs to be loved.

No matter what our needs fulfilled,
Shall happen by the end,
Our bond is everlasting, and
She is my last best friend.

Edward Bowman

PASSING TIME

I thought that if I died today,
I wonder what would be.
What time would pass until each day,
You never thought of me?

I guess it would not matter much,
For I would be beyond,
The Earth and any feelings that,
One might define as fond.

The way our lives are intertwined,
Now gives me daily hope,
This bond of ours will all survive,
With its eternal scope.

It seems each day when I arise,
You are within my mind.
The fondest thoughts and need for you,
Throughout each second wind.

And then when I drift off to sleep,
In comfort of my bed,
I smile as I close my eyes,
And you dance in my head.

In dreams, when I am fast asleep,
I notice you are there.
And see us for the other made,
A Pixie and her Bear.

So, if I were to die today,
I know just what would be.
You'll always know this gentle bond,
And what you mean to me.

PERFECT SCENE

Your head upon my shoulder lays,
My arm around your slender waist.
I think about the different ways,
This scene lets me perfection taste.

The fragrance of the softest hair,
Arises in me to evoke,
The feeling that while you are there,
There's nothing that can ill invoke.

Your gentle breathing next to me,
Hypnotic in its steady pace,
Becalms my thoughts so I can be,
At peace with mind that does not race.

You hear my heartbeat in your ear,
It skips sometimes, but still beats true.
I feel you smile - you have no fear.
You know that it beats just for you.

You whispered something lost to me,
But blame me not, I had no choice.
For I was most fulfilled, you see,
Just by the sound of your sweet voice.

I sigh, contented, with the thought,
That this great moment is quite real.
It feels just like perfection ought,
That when together we both feel.

But tears unbidden start to rise,
Because I notice then your hand,
I try to blink them from my eyes,
And stay within this moment grand.

I see on it the silver ring,
My mind is waking now apace,
My thoughts catch such a simple thing,
That you did tarnished ring replace.

'Twas then I knew all was a dream,
And perfect moment fades away,
Things never will be as they seem,
I wake to face the coming day.

Although all moments finally end,
And sadness sometimes starts anew,
I wished to share with my best friend,
A perfect moment spent with you.

PERFECTION

GOD said that you would have some flaws,
But there are none I see.
When I see you I know that you
Are perfect as can be.

I thought that there would be a point,
As we spend all our time,
That I would see some minor flaw,
Though you were still sublime.

I thought I might with closer look,
And subtle details read,
Detect the slightest flaw in you.
I started with your head.

In glory, it is flaxen crowned,
With soft and flowing hair.
A lovely scent proceeds from it,
And wafts upon the air.

I then look into both your eyes,
Green windows to your soul.
I lose myself within their depths,
And find I'm swallowed whole.

I see your full and soft pink lips,
And think on them awhile.
As I look on, their corners twitch.
You break into a smile.

Your smile grants me life again.
I linger on your face.
Proportions perfect, beautiful,
And emanating grace.

And to your shoulders does your neck,
With gentlest of arcs,
Proceed with beauty delicate,
And deep emotion sparks.

Perfection, too, is evident
In all your body's curves.
Proportioned in an ideal way,
My wonder it deserves.

I think about your caring hands,
Bestowing gentle touch.
The healing power held therein,
Can overcome so much.

So, from a standpoint physical,
I see perfection there.
I thought, therefore, I'll look beyond
Your perfect eyes and hair.

Three things there are that I must have
To stay at woman's side.
If she is sweet, and smart, and strong,
With her I will abide.

I talk with you most every day,
And always am impressed.
Your intellect is vast indeed,
And in you I am blessed.

To know that you have inner strength.
This I can tell with ease.
To weaker women I am not
Attracted, if you please.

Now sweetness deals with character,
And treating one with love.
The essence of what makes you you?
Your Spirit from above.

I looked into your limpid eyes,
The windows to your soul,
And fell into their gentle warmth.
Your depth did me console.

I noticed there an ancient bond,
Connecting you to me.
I wondered how it came about,
And what else I would see.

I saw your soul filled up with love,
And also with the light.
Your perfect soul confronted me,
And gave to me my sight.

Some tears escaped my shuttered eyes,
As I thought about you.
In joy I live because I found,
You're perfect through and through.

GOD said that you would have some flaws,
But there are none I see.
In gratefulness I know you were
Made perfectly for me.

QUESTIONS

Was I lost deep within your eyes,
Or had I just been found,
The moment I fell in the skies,
With feelings so profound?

Was I transfixed by flaxen hair,
Soft soft to gentle touch,
Or did I just caress the air
And not your locks so much?

Was it your lips so full and soft,
That stilled my beating heart,
Or did a rose's petals oft
Life to my soul impart?

Was it your keen intelligence,
That made me love each day,
Or did I have need to convince
You by my side to stay?

Was it your grand complexity,
That kept me entertained,
Or could there other reasons be,
That I by you remained.

The answers to these questions can,
Be answered all in one.
How can you so affect a man,
And how was this begun?

Was it your eyes, lips, hair or brain,
That gives to us such roles?
No, I will by your side remain,
Due to our bonded souls.

SENSES

I notice you are always there.
I feel your presence every day.
In answer to an unsaid prayer,
You came to me and came to stay.

I think about the passing years,
And cannot say when it did start.
Have I seen all your joys and tears?
Have you been always in my heart?

If by ill fate apart we are,
I need to only close my eyes,
To realize you are never far,
And feel the bond that our souls tie.

So beautiful you are to me.
How soft must be your perfect lips?
Your legs and waist both meet, I see,
In gentle curve of lovely hips.

And then I see your shining smile,
Like light that warms from summer skies.
We both know that for quite a while,
I've fallen in your limpid eyes.

So filled my vision is with you,
I know I need no other choice.
I feel awash with feelings true,
And listen to your lovely voice.

I feel emotion well in me,
As dulcet tones caress my ears.
I hope that you will always see,
That we, together, quell all fears

And when we touch in fond embrace
I feel your frame right next to me,
In this I feel your greatest grace,
That I will your protector be.

I gently touch, with great respect,
The softness of your wondrous hair.
This does my inner man affect,
For it is like caressing air.

Again, with reverential care,
For you are perfect in my sight,
I gently touch your flaxen hair,
And note a scent like golden light.

I also sense your light perfume.
It makes my heart some beats to skip,
This scent means that you're in the room,
And I can keenly feel your grip.

I taste the salt within your tears,
As I each one will kiss away,
Together we will face your fears,
For just like you, I came to stay

I cannot help but in you find,
That which no other has fulfilled.
Our spirits are both are intertwined,
And you have all my senses filled.

SORRY

I'm sorry that you could not be,
By my warm fire next to me.
I'd give you Cocoa in a cup,
You'd smile as I filled it up.

And in a blanket soft would I,
Wrap you so gently you might cry,
At such affection that I'd show,
You'd bask within my fire's glow.

Then next we would just watch the flame,
And I'd tell you, I'm glad you came.
Then we would talk throughout the night,
And laugh and share 'til almost light.

You'd fall asleep in cushioned chair,
With smile for your protective bear.
The firelight upon your face,
Illuminates your perfect grace.

So that is how an evening is,
With certain bear and fire his.
I hope that now you might just see,
I'm sorry you're not here with me.

SOUL MATES

Could it be that it always was,
That we together bound have been?
This seems the truth, indeed, because
We both cannot remember when

There was a time we did not know,
That we were one half of a whole.
As if the LORD in mighty blow,
Upon HIS anvil of the soul

Made kindred spirits out of one.
Two people, but with gentle bond,
Yet strong that we to other run,
And cannot help but to be fond.

I look inside the way it seems,
And find I must protector be,
But also want her of my dreams,
To know how much she means to me.

I sometimes wonder, "Does she feel,
The same emotion in her stir?"
I just know nothing is so real,
As my eternal bond to her.

SUFFICIENT

I understand the nature of,
This journey known as life.
Sometimes each breath is drawn in pain,
Because of horrid strife.

And also have I found there is,
Upon the path we trod,
Uneven stones and jagged rocks,
To trip us as we plod.

It seems, though, I have really found,
Someone to walk with me.
Together, both we comfort give,
And travel both as we.

Protecting her from spiteful rocks,
I keep her in my sight,
While she inspires and provides,
Us both with bless-ed light.

I'm humbled for my time with her,
Is beyond any price.
Whatever circumstance shall come,
Her pure love will suffice.

Edward Bowman

SYMBOLS

I. The River

We do not know the time we get,
To live and love upon the Earth.
We always owe the final debt,
And start to die at once from birth.

So, Life the mighty river flows,
In one direction silently,
And no one living ever knows,
How many miles to the sea.

The boats upon this river grand,
Must make the trip with allies few.
I'm grateful for good fortune's hand,
That I will make the trip with you.

II. The Flower

A purple flower in a field,
That I see clearly in my mind,
Suggests to me a love concealed,
And two lives that are intertwined.

Yet every flower speaks to me,
Of even fairer beauty still,
I know it's you that they all see,
And even their dreams you fulfill.

The flowers every year will bloom,
And all their beauty you will see,
I hope when I sleep in my tomb,
That they'll help you remember me

III. The Forest

How many times the paths we trod,
In wooded beauty by the stream?
With scenes designed for us by GOD,
We walked within a Forest dream.

When I, alone, walk 'neath the trees,
I hear them gently all proclaim,
And as they sway within the breeze,
I hear them whispering your name.

Where e'er on Earth you choose to roam,
Whenever you can see a tree,
Be it far distant or at home,
I hope you will remember me.

IV. The Light

Without light we our way can't see,
We seek it all our many years.
Without it we can never be,
Free from our doubt and awful fears.

Since we first met, you've been a source
Of light to help me find my way,
Reflecting light from GOD, of course,
It is your light that starts my day.

I know that I will have to go,
One day from Earth to up above.
I hope that you remember though,
That where your light goes so does love.

V. The Sun

The sun was made to rule the day,
And we rejoice in warmth we feel.
It brings us joy on golden ray,
And does its best our wounds to heal.

I turn my face up to the sun,
And let its warmth wash over me.
My mind goes blank, and I am one,
But with its warmth your face I see.

Wherever you go of a day,
Before the day comes to an end,
A moment take in warmth to stay,
And spare a thought for an old friend.

VI. The Moon

How sacred is the gentle night,
Which moon rules in romantic ways?
It gives to us the softest light,
And with emotions expert plays.

I look up in the nighttime skies,
And wonder if you see it too?
Where e'er you are, do your sweet eyes,
See it and know I think of you?

The moon will my life long outlast,
But I hope it will always be,
That it reminds you of the past,
And fondly you'll remember me.

VII. The Clothes

It seemed to be a pleasant way,
That I could my affection show,
Supplied with outfits of the day,
We had more fun than most will know,

Perchance you never will realize,
The happiness you give to me.
When I behold you with my eyes,
And one of these is what I see.

And for your part, I hope you smile,
With closet bursting at the seams,
And you will think for just a while,
That maybe I fulfilled some dreams

VIII. The Necklace

The pendant spoke to us in stone,
Some diamonds and a tourmaline,
A white gold chain was the capstone,
To show regard for Novalene.

Each time I see you wearing this,
It makes me glad and I feel whole.
I think that maybe I feel bliss,
'Cause it contains part of my soul.

I think you like to wear it out,
If color palette is a match,
I hope of it you think about,
And to it tenderness attach.

IX. The Ring

It seems like such a simple thing,
A piece of metal circled round,
But more than others, with a ring,
A special sentiment is found.

I see the circle broken not,
Which doesn't have a start nor end.
It represents the fairest thought,
Of love I bear for my best friend.

In my life I have four rings bought,
For they, to me, a heart command,
To know you are a constant thought,
Just look down at your own right hand.

X. Epilogue

So many symbols all around,
Their hidden meaning in disguise.
For their sweet message to be found,
We have to look with better eyes.

TACTILE WISTFULNESS

I gently touched her flaxen hair.
A shiver through my body ran.
Its sweetest scent perfumed the air,
And made of me a fulfilled man.

I lightly touched her graceful neck,
And felt her pulse beneath soft skin.
Emotions in my mind a wreck,
For she, the foremost of women.

My hand then drifted down her arm,
Traced supple skin down to her hand.
She put to rest any alarm,
And sifted me like shifting sand.

My eyes took in her yellow top,
With pink straps running underneath.
Protecting both and giving stop,
To fondest treasures soon bequeathed.

My heart now met hers in its pace,
They beat as one in bond profound.
My eyes beheld her beauteous face,
And eyes as green as they were round.

And so I fell into her eyes,
My hand caressing stately cheek.
My fondness now not in disguise,
My inmost man both strong and weak.

I closed my eyes and nearer drew,
And took her breath in lovely sips.
Like beauty of the morning dew,
The touch of soft and yielding lips.

Edward Bowman

TEARS OF JOY

I wept not for the ending world,
I wept not for the falling stars.
I wept not for the quaking Earth,
I wept not for the burning cars.

I wept not for impending doom.
I wept not for consuming fire.
I wept not for the flooding seas,
I wept not for a feeling dire.

I wept because I felt a hand,
I wept because I turned to see.
I wept for joy for what I saw,
I wept for you were still with me.

THE BEAUTY OF US

We went through most our lives, it seems,
Both unaware of what would be.
Yet we kept close our precious dreams,
Though we thought these we'd never see.

At last we met when time was right,
It seems, according to a plan.
I found a woman made of light,
And you found a protective man.

So quickly very close we grew,
Immersed in this new link we found.
We both were grateful for we knew,
That we somehow were gently bound.

Together we discovered things,
That some might call coincidence,
But woven with so many strings,
A tapestry planned made most sense.

We soon realized that every day,
We wanted to together be,
To close beside the other stay,
And light our paths that we might see.

Then we discovered something rare.
That since we were in other's heart,
And each a half of loving pair,
We never really are apart.

It seems a miracle to me,
That all of this has happened thus.
For something wondrous came to be,
A beauty that we know as Us.

THE CLIMB

I looked up to the mountaintop,
And saw her standing there.
A study in exquisiteness,
With flowing, flaxen hair.

Her hair was wafting with a breeze,
While she looked down below.
I knew I had to get to her,
But knew not how to go.

I picked my way up rocky cliff,
And chanced a fatal fall.
To be next to her is a goal,
Worth any risk at all.

I made it to a ledge below,
That was within 10 feet
Of where she waited up above,
For me to climb complete.

The slope was steep and filled with rocks,
Both loose and very sharp.
I took great hope that nearly done
Was climb up brutal scarp.

I tried to climb directly up,
But slid back down the scree.
The jagged stones cut where they touched,
But did not dissuade me.

She looked at me with liquid eyes,
That looked like pools of green.
I found I lost myself in them,
As if she were my queen.

She smiled and she spoke to me,
In a most gentle voice.
She said, "With one more try you'll get
To me, and we'll rejoice.

You see, 'Twas you who put me here,
Up here where I can view,
All things that happen down below,
With no one else but you.

You also let me walk to you,
Upon a stormy sea.
'Tis also in your power to
Complete your climb to me."

So, then I tried to climb again,
While basking in her glow,
She lifted me with her goodwill,
And bade my pain let go.

So stood atop the mountain there,
A queen and loyal knight.
He offers her devotion, and
She gives to all her light.

THE EMBRACE

I promised her that I would try,
For her a daunting task complete.
It took a month, to change apply,
And she did for me something sweet.

She took me in a fond embrace,
How exquisite, her lightest touch,
'Twas filled with gentleness and grace.
How beautiful to be held such.

Her head lay up against my chest,
She must have heard my quickened heart,
I knew that few would be so blessed,
To have her such a gift impart.

I smelled the fragrance of her hair,
And felt her arms around my side.
I wanted to be ever there,
And for this moment to abide.

I felt emotion start to stir,
And blinked the tears back from my eyes.
My universe contained in her,
This angel from beyond the skies.

I do not know how long we stood,
But finally embrace did end.
I think that we both understood,
How deep our bond to other friend.

There is none like her on the Earth,
And something diff'rent is in store,
For never since my ancient birth,
Has one had on me effect more.

THE FIRST TIME

The first time that I you beheld,
You sat upon a chair.
I came out of my office and
I saw you sitting there.
My heart stopped momentarily,
As also did my gait.
My insides filled with butterflies,
The start of something great.

The first time I beheld your form,
I very nearly wept.
Alluring curves moved me within.
My heart within me leapt.
I held my breath because in you,
Perfection did I see.
I realized that I now beheld,
Pure femininity

The first time I looked in your eyes,
I lost myself in them.
Like two pools, clear and cool, I find,
I want to in them swim.
Now every time I close my eyes
It's always yours I see.
Two windows to a perfect soul,
So meaningful for me.

The first time that I felt your touch
I felt a certain thrill.
Like touching a live wire and
Thus being shocked until,
Your touch departed from my frame.
I found I could not breathe,
Though I now blessed amongst mankind,
Should I emotion sheathe?

The first time I beheld your light,
So pure and full of love.
Reflecting perfect divine glow,.
I thank GOD up above.
I'm drawn to bask within your warmth,
As a moth to a flame.
Because you share your inner light,
You lend and love the same.

The first time I realized you care
For me as your true friend,
I felt the tears well in my eyes,
As I felt joy within.
I found with you a special thing,
A bond pure and profound.
How lovely that so firm a link,
Would be so gently bound.

Now every time I think of you,
And all these things I wrote,
A realization strikes me and
I feel I must take note.
That every day, where'er I go,
You're there to quench my thirst.
Each time that I experience you,
It's just like time the first.

THE LADY IN RED

I got a message just today,
I know just who it's from!
Whene'er I see something from her,
She does my heart strings strum.

With joy I opened message up,
And found a pic within.
The picture grew to a great size,
And then I fell therein.

It seemed that I was in a room.
A fog obscured the ground.
The fog also the walls obscured,
But light was all around.

I heard her step before I saw
The vision of her form.
Her footfalls delicate as if
Her walk on clouds the norm.

She moved with grace, which made the fog,
Begin to dissipate.
The last tendrils caressing her,
Ere she did them ablate.

She smiled at me and struck a pose,
Her hand upon her hip.
With one leg straight and one leg bent,
I had to bite my lip.

For standing now in front me
A feminine display,
Perfect in beauty and in grace.
My world just fades away,

Because I look upon her form,
And feelings in me stir,
I realize that my universe,
Is all contained in her.

Her shoes are lovely and are black,
And made in such a way,
To shapely legs accentuate,
And take men's breath away.

The dress is red with hemline short.
It falls high on her thighs,
And further shows her perfect legs,
A blessing to my eyes.

The dress is made with gentle lace,
Which one can just see through.
But opaque slip against her skin,
Obscures the perfect view.

It hints at but does not reveal,
The treasures that men seek.
It shows without unmasking all,
A beautiful physique.

I feel emotions storm inside,
They clash in brutal war.
The fact that she affects me so,
I cannot long ignore.

This only takes a moment, then
I look upon her face.
She smiled as she looked at me,
A visage filled with grace.

She steps toward me, and I toward her,
To seek a fond embrace,
But I slip through the solid floor,
And fall far from that place.

I close my eyes as down I fall,
And think about her hair.
How beautiful and soft it is,
It feels as soft as air.

I realize that it now has stopped,
My plummet from the skies.
I bravely seek to face my fate,
And open up my eyes.

I find I'm sitting in my chair,
Still looking at her form.
Aware of something in my heart,
Both pleasant and quite warm.

I close the picture, but I think
About her once again,
That by her nature she becomes,
Desired by all men.

Edward Bowman

THE NATURE OF DESIRE

On bended knee he searches skies,
To see if there the answer lies.
He wonders, does she realize,
How she his heart made grow in size?
For in it she a place has found.
Marked by a bond deep and profound.

In humbleness he always tries
To earn the gaze of soulful eyes.
Too precious that for which he yearns,
'Tis not a thing that someone earns.
He only by her will be blessed,
And thereby put his heart to rest.

THE PERFECT DAY

We climbed a steep and verdant hill
Nearby where we are wont to walk.
Just like the famous Jack and Jill,
But tumbling not - engaged in talk.

We spread a blanket on the top,
And sat together in the sun.
A friendship that would never stop,
Our gentle bond second to none.

I saw her hair waft in the breeze,
And caught the scent upon the air.
Her presence puts my soul at ease,
I hope she knows how much I care.

I looked into her lovely eyes,
And felt emotion start to grow.
Reflected they the sunlit skies,
They raised my yearning long ago.

I closed my eyes to quell the tears,
And to the sun I turned my face.
I neither feel my pain nor fears,
While basking in her stunning grace.

We watched the clouds move on the wind,
And stories spun from shapes they made.
I wished this day would never end,
But time, alas, its flow obeyed.

As evening fell, she whispered soft
A note of solace in my ear.
By her my Spirit soars aloft,
Does she know how I hold her dear?

We parted then, but for a time,
But I left with her my whole heart.
I know due to our link sublime,
We never really are apart.

THE PERFECT NIGHT

We met at night under the moon,
Which, full, gave bright but gentle light.
On path with lovely petals strewn,
Walked together in the night.

The moon by mist within the air,
Around it had a lighted ring.
The soft light on your softer hair,
My soul, though bound, did closer bring.

As we both walked the path along,
You showed unto me something new.
We listened to a special song.
My universe was only you.

Then romance seized me by the heart,
And logic held in me no sway,
Unbidden by my conscious mind,
My hand to you, then made its way.

It might have gone round slender waist,
Had I not thought before it slid,
That this might be something unchaste,
A touch that you might well forbid.

But then returned my self-control,
And locked my feelings down again.
I smiled for I still felt your soul,
For closer we have never been.

My hand then dropped back to my side,
And I engaged again in talk.
My will again its lock applied,
And finished we romantic walk.

I know that I'm not made of stone,
And that night is a memory,
Of how things have between us grown,
And all that you now mean to me.

THE POET'S DAUGHTER

Delighting in my secrecy,
Each line I write a mystery,
Becomes more clear so one may see,
Or hope to figure out from me,
Regarding what this poem might be,
A reference to my daughters three.

However, I must say to you,
Even though I have more than two,
I'm writing of just one. It's true!
Legitimate, the others too,
Endearing reason for this new,
Encrypted poem the youngest drew

No inkling do I think she had
Because I never truth unclad.
Obscured by pen name ironclad,
We found she liked my verse a tad.
Ere she knew who I am, I'm glad.
Now she knows poet is her dad.

Edward Bowman

THE POWER OF WE

I had a thought occur to me
While waiting for a bus.
Like all the other things in life,
It made me think of us.

I saw these humans passing close,
Embroiled in problems theirs,
And no one seemed to raise their eyes
Weighed down by worldly cares.

I wish no one would be alone;
But be like you and me.
It just takes thinking less of I,
And caring more for We.

TIMELESS

For eons we have been a pair.
The pretty Pixie and her bear.
Also a wizard and his queen,
Their towers in the wood of green.

And yet she also is a dove,
Bound to an owl with perfect love
The owl must her protector be,
So she can fly and know she's free.

These metaphors all ring as true,
But this truth describes something new.
No matter what we face or do,
Throughout all time it's me and you.

Edward Bowman

TOGETHERNESS

You might not know, but every day,
With bated breath I wait for you,
To interact and light my way,
As we find what we both shall do.

I care not for which circumstance,
Nor how we choose our time to spend.
I just know that I need the chance,
To be with you, my dearest friend.

When I look back o'er all the years,
There's no one else like you I see.
With joy you fill to point of tears,
No other means so much to me.

I sometimes wonder how you feel,
But since you also come each day,
And with me precious moments steal,
It seems you might think the same way.

So, everyday a truth grows more,
If even just us in your car,
This truth profound became a core:
Fulfillment mine is where you are.

TRAVELLING

I'm going on a week long trip,
And I'm not sure just how I feel.
Emotions swirl and in their grip,
I slightly lose my even keel.

I think about the cause of this,
And know its caused by how I view,
The place I find my purest bliss,
Which is the time I spend with you.

This week you blessed me even more,
By letting me in person be,
With you, whether in car or store,
And let me your affection see.

You also gave to me consent,
To get for you a silver band.
Reminding of bond permanent,
When you now look at your right hand.

When I examine what I feel,
I find that I must now take heed,
Of truth that seems to me most real,
That it seems you are who I need.

So on this trip, while I'm away,
And many wondrous sights I'll see,
I will take comfort every day,
That you're now always there with me.

UNBOUND DEVOTION

Unbidden my hand reaches out,
To gently touch her lovely cheek.
My queen erases any doubt,
That she is all that I should seek.

Her bearing regal, chin aloft,
A stronger woman won't be found.
Though still most feminine and soft,
She made the strongest to her bound.

I find myself upon my knees,
And reaching toward her pleasant form.
She is now all that my eye sees,
A harbor for me, safe and warm.

I feel in deep emotion drowned,
And see her there within my heart.
And something else me does astound:
I know it happened at the start.

She purses now her regal lips,
A hint of smile starting there.
She stands with hands upon her hips,
Then brushes back her long blond hair.

She reaches out and bids me rise.
My life has now by her been crowned.
I'm held forever in her eyes,
For my devotion is unbound.

UNWORLDLY INFLUENCE

At times the World comes crashing in,
Its only motivation hate.
It seeks to knock me down again,
My head unbowed, with bleeding pate.

For source of strength I look around,
And tears of joy start in my eyes.
I'm saved from bleeding on the ground.
I see you, and I now realize

When I see you approach with grace,
Your form so feminine just flows.
A smile comes to my bruised face,
You stand by me to World oppose.

I feel the texture of your hair,
So soft and long, a perfect frame.
It feels like I caress the air,
And sets my saddened heart aflame.

You take my hand into to your own,
And help me get back to my feet.
The softness of your skin alone,
Gives me the will to World defeat.

I'm grateful that I'm close to you,
And I around you put my arm.
With deepest bond we know it's true,
I'll also keep you safe from harm.

When I look into your clear eyes,
I take unto my soul your light.
I know you're near and I realize,
That everything will be alright.

WAKING UP

It seemed I had a good night's sleep.
I started to awake.
My closed eyes let the senses more
An inventory take.

I heard her breathing next to me,
Content and still asleep.
The even rhythm of her breath,
Described a slumber deep.

I smelled her fragrance in the air,
A feminine perfume.
The lightest aromatic hint
Of sweetness filled the room.

I felt her body next to mine
As I became awake.
Her heart was beating next to mine.
It made my own heart ache.

I felt her head upon my arm,
And softest flowing hair.
My hand caressed her supple skin.
I overflowed with care.

My consciousness now fully there,
I opened up my eyes,
And looked upon such beauty that,
I thought that I might die.

The morning sun set fire to
Her long and pretty hair.
It also showed perfection in
Her body laying there.

Her face had such a symmetry,
Perfectly feminine.
Even without her makeup on,
Her beauty drew me in.

I gently touched her on the cheek.
She smiled with surprise.
She softly purred in morning stretch,
Then opened up her eyes.

Emotions raw were then released,
From deep within my soul.
I knew that she had taken me,
And had me swallowed whole.

I felt a wave wash over me.
The room became a blur.
I knew then that my universe
Is all contained in her.

I feel a profound gratefulness,
To her who did me see.
She saw past all my many faults,
And showed me high esteem.

Wherever I might look in life,
I cannot help but see,
This woman who is filled with love,
And who awakened me.

WHAT I FOUND

While walking on a wooded lane,
I saw you in the sweetest bow'r,
So happy was I at my gain,
I found in you a perfect flow'r.

I know that I created was,
To be protector, as a rule,
With you I felt this more because,
I found in you a precious jewel.

I see you demonstrate your might,
As life tries happiness to kill,
You never lose romantic sight,
I found in you an iron will

When we choose to together walk,
And spending time, we both connect,
I'm mindful every time we talk
I found in you great intellect

My days before were shades of gray,
A slow descent into the night,
But you brought me a brand new day,
I found in you a source of light

Each day I'm grateful that you're there.
My thankfulness will never cease.
My life complete, No more despair.
I found in you the missing piece

We tell each other secret things,
And spend our hours without end,
Just seeing what each talk will bring.
I found in you my greatest friend.

Together we are drawn it seems,
And as you know I've grown quite fond.
We fuel each other's hopes and dreams.
I found in you a special bond

For my part, I will always know,
That you were sent from GOD above.
Although, sometimes, it might not show,
I found in you someone to love.

WHAT MAKES HER BEAUTIFUL

How beautiful her eyes that see,
Past all of my faults,
To the goodness in me.

How beautiful her flaxen hair,
That favors my dreams,
And is softer than air.

How beautiful her lips so sweet
That rivals a rose,
With soft petals replete.

How beautiful her touch so soft,
That takes me when down,
To then bear me aloft.

How beautiful her perfect grace,
That gives me great hope,
When I look on her face.

How beautiful her inner light,
That lights up my path,
And disperses my night.

How beautiful she is to me.
She makes everything,
In my life better be.

How beautiful her ancient soul,
That's bound to my own,
As two halves of a whole.

WONDER

I sometimes wonder what you see,
Or think of when you look at me.
Am I, to you, a special man,
Or just another loving fan.

I sometimes wonder at the thought,
That you are something I'd not sought.
Do you not feel the gentle bond,
That joins us both in feelings fond?

Perhaps you might already know,
Because I do my fondness show,
I can't deny that it is true,
The wonder that I found in you.

Edward Bowman

WORTH THE WAIT

When trials all about me press,
And dark obscures my sight.
It gives me strength to know that she,
Will give to me her light.

I wait for her to come to me,
Down from her lofty height,
Perfection found in her complete,
Her raiment spotless white.

Now every time she comes to me,
And fills me with delight,
I hold her in a fond embrace,
And everything seems right.

And should she ever need defense,
Or is pressed in a fight.
I will be there whene'er she calls,
And give to her my might.

SHUTTERING THE FORGE

I had been working at my forge,
And shaping things by art
I had no plans nor schedule. I
Just simply used my heart.

I made some pretty pieces, and
My patron did concur.
This raised me up because, in truth,
They all were made for her.

One day as I was hard at work,
She stood right next to me.
She smiled and I thought that I
Might nothing fairer see.

My hammer might have struck it poor,
For anvil rang not true,
And from it came an untoward piece,
A bifurcated view.

You see, I saw the work as good,
All but the end, I thought.
But still the piece was most intact,
To plan that I had wrought.

I should have thrown it in the forge,
To smelt it once again.
Instead I thought though slightly flawed
She would see good within.

The thing that one must keep in mind,
About an artist's work,
Is that with him this duty lies,
And it he cannot shirk.

The artist is responsible
For what the viewer feels,
And leading Patron through the work
To place that is ideal.

I meant the piece as general,
A reference to mankind,
And what we all find beautiful,
And what we seek to find.

I must have been too close to it,
When hammer anvil struck,
And blinded by the sparks that flew,
I saw not my bad luck.

I saw the disappointment flash
Across my patron's face.
And let the piece fall to the ground,
To be swept from this place.

I realized I'd been standing there,
For some amount of time.
I dropped the hammer from my hand,
And saw it was nighttime.

I shuttered, then, the massive forge,
To let the fire go out.
I swept and put the tools away,
And left without a doubt.

I would be back to use my forge,
As I was meant to do.
I still had much unfinished work,
That she had yet to view.

With fifteen pieces started now,
And four books not yet done.
I will continue in my work,
When next I see the sun.

ABOUT THE AUTHOR

Edward Bowman grew up in the St. Louis metropolitan area on the Illinois side of the river. He has always had an interest in the arts. In addition to writing, he also enjoys music and painting. He met his Muse in Indiana while on assignment writing documentation for software for a development house. He and Aurora keep in touch and see each other when they can. He still lives by the mighty Mississippi, in Missouri, on his small farm with his horse and four dogs.

ABOUT THE MUSE

Aurora Dawn was born and raised on Cayman Brac in the Caribbean. Since her family could trace their lineage back to royalty, and her name lent itself to such interpretation, she lightheartedly became known as "Princess" to friends and family. She traveled extensively for the software company she represented, and always seemed to leave people happier than she found them. She met Edward in Indiana when the company needed her there for an upcoming release. After finishing this assignment, she returned to her Caribbean home via cruise ship. She lives in a house by the beach with her cat, Biscuit.

www.ingramcontent.com/pod-product-compliance
Lightning Source LLC
Chambersburg PA
CBHW031317040426
42443CB00005B/107